Revised Edition

HIRE
Amazing
EMPLOYEES

What Others Are Saying ...

"I've preached this for over 20 years: Hire for character and fit, train for skills and experience! You—and your hires—will both be happier and more productive! It starts with a well-designed strategic selection system as outlined in *Hire Amazing Employees, Revised Edition.*"
— John W Howard PhD,
CEO, Performance Resources, Inc.

"When hiring people, most of us still rely upon the traditional hiring approach: resume strength, interview success, and references. What's missing? Good quality data! It's objective information that gives us the whole picture. Take away sole reliance upon 'gut-feel,' and you will hire people who can achieve real results and positively impact your bottom line."
—BB, President, management software

"I've been frustrated, when hiring employees, countless times in my 30-year career. After working with Jeannette and using her techniques, I felt empowered. I hired employees who fit their jobs and improved the quality of our deliverables! I've never seen a better, more comprehensive plan for achieving success through hiring the right person for the right job."
—JH, CEO, technology development

"*Hire Amazing Employees* is a book that needs to be read by all business owners with employees and HR managers. It is a fast read and full of great information. Jeannette Seibly gets right to the point and provides information about all aspects of hiring employees from where to find great employees to how to conduct a thorough interview. I highly recommend this book if you are looking for practical and easy ways to hire the right employee the first time!"

—Amazon Reviewer

Also by Jeannette L. Seibly ...

Selected business books:

Hire Amazing Employees, Second Edition:
Improve Your Profits and Your Work Life!

It's Time to Brag! Business Edition

The Secret to Selling Yourself Anytime, Anywhere:
Start Bragging!

Be a Podcast Guest (and get invited back!)

Fiction books:

The Old Wooden Rocker
A Mother's Greatest Regret

Books are available on Amazon.com, B&N, and in
independent bookstores everywhere (*SeibCo.com*).

SeibCo, LLC

Interested in quantity discounted purchases for company
training, promotions, and educational needs? Contact
Jeannette Seibly @ JLSeibly@SeibCo.com for details.

Leadership, selection, coaching, and management articles
written by Jeannette Seibly are available on her website,
SeibCo.com. You can also sign up to receive her weekly
blog, *Entrepreneurial Leaders.*

HIRE
Amazing
EMPLOYEES

How to Increase Retention, Revenues and Results!

Jeannette L. Seibly

MOUNTAIN
OWL
PRESS

Hire Amazing Employees, Revised Edition:
How to Increase Retention, Revenues and Results!

This book is designed to provide information related to the subject matter covered. The purpose is to educate. It is sold with the understanding that while these are practical ideas successfully used by many companies and business professionals, neither the author nor the publisher shall have any liability or responsibility to any person or entity with respect to any loss or damage caused, or alleged to be caused, directly or indirectly by the information contained in this book.

This book is the revised edition of *Hire Amazing Employees,* © 2006, 2013 and 2022.

Published by Mountain Owl Press

MOUNTAIN
OWL
PRESS

www.SeibCo.com

ISBN: 978-1-7353504-6-2 (Print)
ISBN: 978-1-7353504-7-9 (eBook)
ISBN: 978-1-7353504-8-6 (Ingram)
Library of Congress Control Number: 2022912964

Editors: Carolyne Ruck, Help-U-Write; and Peggie Ireland with The Book Shepherd

Thank you to contributors Diane Putvin, Jill Tietjen, Bobby Crew, Judith Briles, and John W. Howard, PhD

Book Cover & Layout: Nick Zelinger, NZ Graphics

Printed in the United States of America

CONTENTS

Very Important Note ...

Work with your human resource
professional, business manager, and/or
employment attorney to ensure each step of
your strategic selection system meets legal
requirements for local, state, and federal
(and international where appropriate) statutes.
Remember, different locales may have different
requirements and will indicate when the
information can be obtained
and how it can be used.

Additionally, many jurisdictions prohibit asking
a job candidate about current or past wages
and salaries since they have the effect of
perpetuating gender and racial pay inequity.
Check legal ramifications before asking
a job candidate.

Since she had two hours before she boarded her flight back to Detroit, Jessica chose a seat far away from the airline check-in gate. She needed her time and space for reviewing and sending texts and emails to key people back at the office.

She texted Jacob, president of her company, first:

We're growing. Just added a new hire in the Denver region. Our team did a great job of vetting the final three candidates.

As she hit "send," she heard her name. Looking up, she saw Travis, director for a tech company in Austin, standing next to her. She remembered meeting him in Dallas several years ago at a national tech trade show.

Smiling, she closed her laptop. "Hi. How are you? It's been a while."

"It has been, Jessica." As he sat next to her, he added, "When was the last time we saw one another? Oh …" He snapped his fingers as he remembered—Dallas. "So, where are you heading?"

"Back home to Detroit. What about you?"

"I'm heading to Austin, then on to Phoenix. Busy interviewing people for our company.

"Have time for coffee? Oh … I mean tea," Travis said, remembering Jessica enjoyed a good cup of tea without sugar, unlike how it's made in Texas.

Jessica nodded. "Sure. It will be great to catch up." She'd finish the emails later.

After they were seated in a nearby restaurant, Jessica sipped her tea and asked, "How are the interviews going?"

"You know how it is. Just when you think you've found the right person, someone snatches him or her away with a better offer."

Jessica smiled and nodded. "I remember experiencing that many times in the past. I'm grateful that doesn't happen now. I was here to talk with the final three candidates for our western region office located here in Denver."

"Did you select one?"

Jessica nodded in affirmation. "Job offer made and accepted. She starts in two weeks."

Travis paused, thinking, *what is she doing that I'm not?* "Well ... our hiring and selection system must not be as fine-tuned as yours. I had five interviews scheduled, and only three of them showed! Of the three, only one may have some promise. It's up to our CEO to interview the person before we offer any job. And even though I may like the person, it doesn't mean he will. Henry relies on his gut way too often. We've lost several great candidates because of it. And later he'd ask me why we didn't make them job offers."

"I'm sorry to hear that. It makes recruiting very time-consuming when people don't show," Jessica replied.

"What's your secret—would you share it?" Travis asked.

"Secret?" Jessica replied, looking surprised by the question. "You know ... you jet out here to Denver and talk with three candidates. You're able to select the final one, make a job offer, and have the person accept."

"Hmm...," Jessica was perplexed. "I simply follow our strategic selection system. I only come out after the Denver management staff has interviewed and completed the required due diligence for the final three candidates."

"Oh!" Travis said. "I wish we had one of those. A streamlined process so I could focus on other aspects of my job instead of constantly traveling around the United States interviewing people."

Jessica looked at him, almost amused with his response. "Well ... it definitely does make it easier. Our retention, revenues, and results have improved dramatically over the past three years."

"Really?" Travis asked skeptically.

Jessica nodded.

"So, what's the secret?" Travis asked again.

Jessica took a sip of tea before responding. "Several years ago, we were doing a poor job of hiring people. Really, in hindsight, horrendous. Those hiring mistakes included job transfers and job promotions. Jacob, the owner of our company, operated under the false belief that he could spot talent a mile away. Then, he imagined he could single-handedly train, coach, and manage them for success."

"Let me guess. That wasn't working out too well," Travis said with a half-smile.

"True." Jessica replied. "When our numbers came out halfway through that infamous year, we knew we were in big trouble. Both customer and employee turnover were high, profits were low, and some of our deliverables were late to the customer. Plus, there was customer pushback."

Travis simply nodded, waiting for Jessica to continue.

"So, Jacob hired Judy, an executive business coach. After, a month of working with her, he learned we needed to do a much better job with hiring, job transfers, and job promotions. Jacob then had Judy talk with his vice presidents—all five of us weekly one-on-one."

"That bad, huh?" Travis replied with a frown.

"Yes and no. Yes, we needed it. And, no, it actually was great!" Jessica paused again before finishing her tea while glancing at her phone to check the time. She didn't want to miss her flight and glanced out the window to see if the snowstorm passing through had diminished any.

Seeing a wall of whiteness, she continued, "Judy gathered us into a full day workshop and training session. During that time, we designed a strategic selection system, to identify the most qualified candidates, to the job offer, then through employee orientation and onboarding."

"Wow! Sounds intense."

"Not really. But you're right. At first it seemed overwhelming. There was work to do. A couple of times we had intense *come down to reality* conversations since most of us had been hiring and firing for years. We had relied on our intuition and gut — just like Jacob did. The problem was that method didn't work and we didn't know how to improve what we were doing. As you know, change can be hard, especially when you're busy putting out fires.

"The good news was we started seeing improvement. We attracted new job candidates and everything smoothed out. A couple of months later, we started to see an increase in both new and existing customers due to our improved delivery systems.

"Then, the five of us fell back into old habits when a potential hire looked and talked the part, but the data didn't agree. Judy reminded us to *trust the strategic selection system.* She kicked some executive butt and got us back on track.

"It wasn't easy since we hated change and, initially, like any new habit, we felt the strategic selection system took longer than before. The reality was that it took longer because we were stubborn and resisted following the system. We were reminded that if we hired based on "job fit," we wouldn't be so busy handling the same old problems or firefighting! In the end, once we embraced the changes, the process was smoother and easier than our previous trial-and-error approach."

"Job fit?"

"You know ... getting right people into the right jobs.

"I was pleasantly surprised when we actually got the right people in the right jobs. It did reduce turnover, miscommunication, and team conflict. It's amazing how well the company runs now. We can focus on growing the company instead of continually training new hires and handling the same old complaints from customers."

Skepticism spread across Travis' face. "I find it hard to believe that after spending the last several years on the road interviewing candidates, you'd have immediate results. People will be people. Like you said, some can talk the game, but cannot do the job ... some spin quite the story." Then Travis added, "But I don't know if our company would do that. It sounds time consuming. I mean we have enough disruption occurring right now in our industry. I don't know if we could handle anymore change."

He looked at his watch and said, "I gotta go. My flight is scheduled to board in fifteen minutes. It's been great to reconnect."

At that moment, both heard the announcement that all flights would be delayed for several hours due to the snowstorm moving through Denver.

Travis sat down again, then paused before saying, "You piqued my interest. If we had a more efficient selection and hiring process, it would reduce a lot of the challenges we have working with people who do not fit their jobs. I'd like to learn more about how to create a strategic selection system. Would you spend some time with me and help me improve our selection system? Dinner will be on me."

Jessica hesitated a moment. "Sure. It's not hard. But it does focus on the basics. Are you willing to get back to basics?"

She watched Travis' face change from anticipation to dread.

She continued with a smile, "It's what Judy had us do. Too often, most rely on hiring fads, gimmicks, and other 'hiring tricks.' Qualifications are based on the tiniest bits of information. Candidates are selected for some really irrational reasons, including relying on the old intuition or gut approach."

Travis relaxed and then replied, "Okay, I'm just surprised. I thought you would share some new cutting-edge process. You know, something similar to the technology break-throughs most have experienced in business."

Jessica laughed. "No. Just getting back to the basics. Being clear about who, what, when, where, and why, before getting into the how to get it done."

She paused before adding, "Dinner sounds great, Travis. I'm really hungry for an excellent steak with a superb cabernet."

Both laughed, knowing it would be time well spent.

Introduction

Have you noticed? There's an elephant in the room.

Many business owners, executives, entrepreneurs, and hiring managers find selection a painful process. The unspoken fear of getting it wrong paralyzes many, and others are in denial that a solution even exists. It's the elephant in the room that sabotages them when making hiring, job transfer, or job promotion decisions.

Why do we resist changing?

- Fear of looking incompetent.

- Hiding little or no training as interviewers.

- Hoping customers and top talent won't notice when employees are leaving.

- Fear of saying or doing the wrong thing when talking with "diverse" job candidates.

- Lack of knowledge on how to obtain good and reliable objective data and use it.

- Miscommunication of expectations and forgetting promises made.

- Citing lack of time and money required to follow a well-designed strategic selection system that includes a structured interview approach.

Even with high turnover of top talent and loss of great customers, we hang on to our outdated perceptions that we're doing the best we can.

What's the #1 challenge? The interviewer!

- Once we make up our minds, we are extremely resistant to change.

- We are well-trained to draw conclusions from tiny fragments of information.

- Our perceptions influence our reality and our decisions, and perceptions are naturally flawed.

- We rely on our perceptions to make our selection decisions, only to learn that we made a mistake that has cost us retention, revenues, and results! Our top talent and great customers leave ... many never to return.[1]

I remember interviewing a woman for a human resources position for a client. When I asked her about her experiences designing and using a strategic selection system, her response was, "I have great intuitive skills. I can tell by talking with people for a few minutes whether or not they will be a good fit."

While some of you may agree with her statement, the truth is that you cannot intuitively tell if someone will be a good fit without good, objective data. And your intuition is no defense against lawsuits or the frustration of disgruntled employees and customers having to deal with these bad hires. (Hint: It's why they leave!)

If that doesn't get your attention, here is some information that might:

- We rely mostly on resumes to determine who we will interview, and over 85% have inaccuracies or lies contained in them.[2]

- We rely on our intuition or gut to determine to whom we will provide job offers. This usually occurs within the first 4 to 15 minutes of meeting the job candidate. The balance of the interview time makes no difference! (Such snap decisions are heavily influenced by unconscious bias resulting in unequal treatment for job applicants.)[3]

- We fail to consistently conduct due diligence (background checks, employment and education verifications, employer references) citing they take too much time and won't reveal anything we don't already know!

If you engage in any of these selection practices, and many employers do, there are several legal issues.

- The most important one is you must follow the same process for every candidate being considered for a particular position.

- You never know who is a wolf in sheep's clothing, and the chances of you discovering them is very low!

- Many job applicants are highly adept at talking the talk, parroting back what you want to hear, and looking the part.

This book was written for hiring managers, entrepreneurs, executives in small businesses, and family business leaders who have been wrestling with these elephants and want to make a change when selecting new hires in the United States and internationally.

A more effective strategic selection system will improve the success rate for hiring:

- New Hires
- Rehires
- Remote workers
- Job transfers
- Job promotions
- Contractors or consultants becoming full- or part-time employees

One wrong person selected for the right job (or the right person put in the wrong job) will alter your workplace culture, customer list, and profitability.

When an employee fails so does the company, especially in small businesses since it's harder to hide someone that is not doing the job well. (Many of you can imagine the challenges of having more than one bad hire.)

Elephants can occur at the oddest of times and become ghosts of interviews past! When a company relies on intuitive or gut reactions to determine which candidates to interview and select for positions, it can come back to bite the company's sales and reputation!

As an employer, do you fail to understand or appreciate that when you use poor selection processes, the candidates you ignored or rejected due to biases and faulty practices are the same people who are now in positions to influence whether or not their company will become your customer, vendor, or determine if you receive an award or sales contract?

It's Time to Get Back to Basics

Basic skills in anything are a prerequisite to mastering advanced skills, but they are also a solid foundation in themselves. And business executives and professionals need to have that grounding in math, writing, and communication as well as those skills essential to their individual business.

You may say, "But I don't need basic skills to be successful." Consider, without good solid, basic skills, you'll be ineffective in addressing your customers' needs, creating new and profitable ideas, and growing your business.

The same is true when it comes to selecting people to get the work done. Too often you spend more time (and money) selecting equipment or technology than in selecting the right people to operate it! It's very costly, time consuming, and hurts your reputation as an employer and service/product provider when you miscalculate! Sadly, you often do!

What's the trap that leads to hiring the wrong person?

Several years ago a business leader said to me, "I simply want people to show up and do their work. I know what needs to be done. They simply need to do what I tell them to do."

This traditional point-of-view needs to be transformed and so must the "intuitive" or "wild, wild west approach" (ad-hoc practices) to selecting employees be changed so companies can succeed.

The problem is two-fold.

1) Many employees today want to have more say in the work they do and how it's done.

2) And, employees often need to make quick decisions and they cannot always run to ask the boss what to do in every situation. (And, would the boss really want employees asking him or her what to do all the time?)

It's time to invest in your hiring and promotion practices. This is how amazing employees are selected and profitable companies experience growth!

A well-designed strategic selection system doesn't happen by accident. It takes an investment of time to collect good objective data, conduct good interviews, and use this information appropriately. This is especially true in small businesses that cannot afford to make the same mistakes that larger companies seem to get away with.

What's an added benefit to using a strategic selection system? When potential employees of questionable quality see a well-defined process and a commitment to following it, they won't stick around to see if you find out their weaknesses. They'll simply move on to their next target ... your competitor! (Just think, they've done you a favor!)

Be slow to hire and faster to fire by using your strategic selection system on a consistent and on-going basis!

A business owner in the healthcare industry set up a strategic selection system to ensure she had great key employees. Then, she stopped using it once she believed she had all of her critical positions filled. When asked why, she replied, "I won't need it anymore. I've hired great employees!"

She was surprised when employees (including key ones) started leaving and taking her customers with them. But when sustainable business practices and systems are no longer used, mischief happens!

Since *Hire Amazing Employees, Second Edition* was released in 2013, there have been many nefarious practices developed to attract, hire, and retain top talent. With so many changes in laws (local, state, and federal, and international if hiring abroad), you need to ensure you're up-to-date legally and using the best tools available. It's the best defense when someone files a lawsuit (and sadly, there is a lot of employment litigation).

But more importantly, when you follow a well-designed strategic selection system, it's the best way to attract and retain amazing employees and great customers! Now, you're hiring, transferring, and promoting the right people!

Still not convinced? Here are some common challenges many hiring bosses' experience. How many can you identify with? Be honest!

- I want people to like me and fear looking like a robot following a system.

- Anyone can do this job (warm body syndrome).

- I believe there are separate interview questions to ask women and people of color.

- I don't need to conduct background checks or honesty/integrity assessments, I can look into the whites of their eyes and know if they are lying or not. (Yes, I've had this mentioned several times by business owners no longer in business.)

- Of course, the major culprits are ego, mindset, and busyness. ("I have it all handled." OR "I don't need a system; I'll know the person when I meet him/her.")

- Bad hiring habits learned from previous bosses or online forums.

- I've been doing "intuitive hiring" for many years and have never had a problem. (Bosses are unaware of the issues their team members and customers grapple with due to "bad" hires.)

- Employees are promoted too soon without the required training and job fit (think, low customer satisfaction and low employee morale).

- There are not different career ladders available for employees wanting new jobs or paycheck opportunities that does not require managing people.

- Subtle changes occur when contractors or consultants become full- or part-time position employees.

- There is a false belief that it takes too much time and costs too much to create a well-designed strategic selection system. (A common excuse: "I'm too busy putting out fires and keeping the customers happy.")

All these excuses get in the way of attracting and keeping top talent, being profitable, and delivering exceptional results to customers.

The most often overlooked issue is the cost of placing people in the wrong jobs, also known as hiring mistakes. It's tremendous! Since most companies do not have a line item or other method to track the true cost of hiring mistakes or selection errors, there is an insidious drain of resources occurring until it can no longer be ignored.

It's like a slow oil leak that you don't notice until the indicator light on your vehicle dashboard lights up, warning you to get it handled NOW! But why wait until disaster strikes? The cost will be much greater!

When you use a well-designed strategic selection system and avoid one bad hire, it will more than pay for your updates or upgrades!

- Countless research confirms that those who fit their jobs produce more, stay longer, and help create happier workplaces.

- The modern workforce is more diverse and transient, and desires a better work/life balance.

- Technology allows people to work from anywhere.

- International hires are increasing for a variety of reasons.

Welcoming these changes creates new opportunities! It requires focusing on hiring, transferring, and promoting the right people to create a profitable, diverse, and sustainable company.

Gender and ethnic diversity correlates with profitability and speaks well for companies that focus on hiring for diversity.[4]

The main reasons you need a well-designed strategic selection system as your foundation are for hiring new employees, rehiring former employees, selecting people who can work remotely, transitioning consultants or contractors into full- or part-time employees, job transfers, and job promotions.

Here are some truisms that are often overlooked. Employees:

- Come to us with their own thinking styles, core behaviors, and occupational motivations/interests.

- Cannot be coached, trained, or motivated to be other than who they are!

- Have goals they want to develop and achieve.

- Want more work/life balance ... and time with their families and friends.

- Wish to pursue life interests and goals.

- Desire to work in a diverse workplace.

- Want to be valued, heard, and trained to take on bigger opportunities.

Now that you know the reasons why the conventional methods of employee selection can have negative results, the remainder of this book, *Hire Amazing Employees: How to Increase Retention, Revenues and Results,* will guide you (or remind you) how to:

- Set up a well-designed strategic selection system and follow it.

- Realize the true cost of hiring mistakes and how a well-designed strategic system is cost-effective.

- Utilize methods and tools that work and meet legal requirements.

- Conduct interviews that make a positive difference.

- Conduct a thorough due diligence designed to elicit and uncover the information required to keep a safe and healthy workplace.

- Choose the right qualified assessments to help determine job fit for selecting the right person for the right job.

The basic ingredients offered in *Hire Amazing Employees, Revised Edition* draws on decades of experience and practice, including some hard lessons learned by my clients and me! I will introduce and/or reinforce practical techniques for hiring, transferring, and promoting top producers based on real-life experiences.

Also, I'll introduce you to the Selection Triad as a way to guide you back to basics. This will improve retention, revenues, and results in your business. And your reputation as a great employer will attract and keep well-deserved customers, improve quality delivery systems, and enhance job satisfaction. Remember, people impact every system and asset within your company! They either run your systems by following the procedures manual or make up their own at the expense of coworkers and customers.

Let's get back to basics and learn how to consistently select the right people for the right jobs (aka job fit). Once you understand the basics, you can build, modify, and adjust your selection system to better meet your needs, and those of your employees and customers.

Happy Hiring!

Jeannette

Jeannette L. Seibly

PS: Warning! Once you've done a great job of hiring amazing employees that fit their jobs, be sure you're a top employer. Keep your company's policies, systems, management practices, strategic goals, training, communication and procedures updated to ensure they remain top-notch.

An Important Reminder ...

Work with your human resource
professional, business manager, and/or
employment attorney to ensure each step of
your strategic selection system meets legal
requirements for local, state, and federal
(and international where appropriate) statutes.
Remember, different locales may have different
requirements and will indicate when
the information can be obtained
and how it can be used.

Additionally, many jurisdictions prohibit asking
a job candidate about current or past wages
and salaries since they have the effect of
perpetuating gender and racial pay inequity.
Check legal ramifications <u>before</u> asking
a job candidate.

Part 1

Foundation of the Selection Triad: Let's Get Started

After each chapter a blank page or two is provided for NOTES. Instead of trying to remember your questions or ideas, I recommend writing them down. It will make the process seem less overwhelming as you go along.

- Chapter 1: The Selection Triad – What Is It and Why Should You Care?

- Chapter 2: Create a Strategic Selection System

- Chapter 3: Costly Mistakes in Hiring, Job Transfers, and Job Promotions

- Chapter 4: Two Key Questions That Must Be Answered for Each Open Position

- Chapter 5: Create a Job Description

- Chapter 6: Create a 180-Day Success Plan

- Chapter 7: Select the Right Applicant Tracking System (ATS) and Learn How to Use It
  - Select the Right ATS for Your Company
  - Create Prescreening Questions
  - Why Employers Should Require That a Full Application Be Completed
  - Important Note About Resumes
  - Keep Job Applicants Engaged

- Chapter 8: Attract Qualified Job Candidates with Job Ads and Job Postings
  - URL or QR Code Link Etiquette
  - Writing Job Ads and Postings that Attract Better Candidates
  - Additional Resources for Job Ads and Postings

- Chapter 9: Use the Right Assessments and Skill Tests
  - Job Candidates Are Like Pyramids
  - To Get Started, Review the Technical Manual
  - Purpose of Reliability vs. Validity and Why It's Critical
  - Use of Cut-Offs with Assessments and Skill Testing
  - Skill Testing
  - Core Value Assessments
  - Job Fit Assessments
  - Job Fit and Job Matching

- Chapter 10: Phone Screen Interview Questions, Full Interview Questions, and Reference Check Questions

Then, you're ready to proceed to Part 2 (Interviews and Assessments), Part 3 (Due Diligence), and Part 4 (The Job Offer and Employee Onboarding).

1

The Selection Triad –
What Is It and Why Should You Care?

Great job fit is the #1 reason people succeed, according to a major study conducted by *Harvard Business Review.*[5]

Do you believe spending more time selecting the right technology is better than creating a well-designed strategic system to select the right employee? Most of you will say, "no."

Many hiring managers today realize poor selection decisions cost a lot of time, money, and customers. However, they are unclear about how to select people based on job fit.

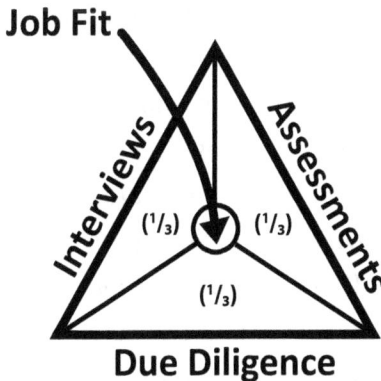

Job Fit

Interviews

Assessments

($1/_3$) ($1/_3$)

($1/_3$)

Due Diligence

Foundation: Critical Prep Work

There are Three Places Where You Can Impact Top Performance: Hiring (or Selection), Skill Development and Training, and Firing.

The least expensive and most effective of these is focusing on hiring/selection for job fit. You increase retention, revenues, and results when designing and following a strategic selection system which consists of critical prep work: interviews, assessments, and due diligence. Then, finally, the job offer!

Why should you care?

Focusing on all three sides of the Selection Triad and the foundation will make the difference between selecting a so-so employee or top talent, losing or keeping customers, and achieving mediocre results or being profitable! It's selecting for job fit!

The right people in the right jobs will impact your retention, revenues, and results, and most importantly, your company's reputation. The results will be reflected in your ability to compete on quality, price, and service of your products and services.

Creating a viable strategic selection system is no different than buying a car. It's a hefty investment, even if you're leasing it. When you look without a plan or specs in mind, you're at the mercy of every persuasive salesperson who is happy to sell you any quality of vehicle on the lot by telling you, "It's a great deal."

Then, the elephants appear. It won't have the quality, functionality, and/or price you need. You will then lose trust in it when something goes wrong (and it will) ... and faith in yourself!

The same is true when you are searching for the right employees. Without a strategic selection system, you will slowly lose confidence in your abilities to hire, transfer, and promote the right people into the right jobs! It doesn't need to be that way.

The key is designing a strategic selection system and trusting the process when following it.

The goal is to ensure the person you interviewed is the same person who shows up on the job, day after day.

After working from both sides of the desk (hiring and being hired as an interviewer and being a job candidate) for over 30 years, I've seen hiring bosses do a five-minute interview and the person is hired or not. I've seen hiring managers conduct long, drawn-out interviews over the course of days, weeks, or months with the same outcome.

The difference with those hired? Not much! The employers still experienced high turnover, miscommunication, and disgruntled employees and customers. The reason? They failed to use a well-designed strategic selection system!

The additional problem? Those not hired were left with a negative experience. They told their friends, family, business associates, and online followers not to do business with that company. And their future employers too!

The good news? This can be avoided when taking the time to create and use a well-designed strategic selection system ... getting back to basics.

Notes ...

Notes …

2

Create a Strategic Selection System

Creating policies and procedures are usually easy for most companies. Many have standard templates for how to format and write a formal system and how to keep it updated.

The challenge for any new system is getting yourself and others to follow it!

Creating a step-by-step system using the right processes and tools will attract qualified candidates and guide you to select the right ones as employees.

To return to the car analogy, evaluating employees is just like looking at vehicles. You'll see that many are impressive. Leather and other extras are enticing. But do they have the functionality, quality, and price that you need and can afford?

A Best Practice for Creating a Strategic Selection System

- Bring together a team of key hiring managers, including human resource person(s).
  (Hint: keep the team small: four to six people.)

- Review company mission, vision, and values. Note: If your company doesn't have these or doesn't follow them, now is NOT the time to create them or reinforce them. It'll cause confusion with both current and future employees. When you decide in the future to create these guiding principles, do it as a separate and formal process that gets everyone on the same page and practicing them daily.

- Visualize what skills/qualities top performers would need, the process of finding them, and results needed for the company.

- Brainstorm ideas (focus on who, what, when, where, and why; stay out of the "how" at this point).

- Create an outline or structure for the system, and only after everyone has aligned with it, fill in the details.

- Create the procedures (aka "how" to make it happen).

- Select the right tools and be sure to conduct BETA testing that includes users (aka job candidates).

Note: I recommend seeking out three vendors for each tool: ATS (Applicant Tracking System), assessments, and background checks. Compare functionality, price, and fit with your company before selecting the best one(s) to use. To get started, ask your industry network, business consultant, and/or executive coach for ideas.

- Fine-tune along the way as some tools may require extra steps not originally included in the system since they were unknown in the initial planning stages.

- Set up intracompany online access so any person responsible for hiring, job transfers, and job promotions can readily access the system and use the policies, procedures, and tools.

- Training is critical! Train ALL hiring managers and hold them responsible and accountable for their hiring results.

I've been surprised that many recruiters and hiring managers don't know what EEO, ADA, and DOL (and other acronyms) stand for. The history and purpose of these federal acts are very important in understanding why a well-designed strategic selection system is required to improve retention, revenues, and results.

Conduct training around these agencies and legislation once a year and don't be afraid to repeat yourself (yes, you'll sound like a parrot) until they can mimic you!

A Quick Note about Working with External Recruiters, Human Resource Consultants, and Vendors

It's important that, when they work with you, they use your strategic selection system instead of allowing them to do it their way. Top performance and productivity occur when everyone is operating on the same page. It ensures consistent, reliable, and quality results for your business and customers.

Be sure to read any contract or agreement and understand it before signing it.

Notes ...

Notes ...

3

Costly Mistakes in Hiring, Job Transfers, and Job Promotions

I remember meeting a former business owner who immediately exclaimed, after I was introduced to him, "I wish I would have met you sooner!"

I asked, "Why?"

His reply was very insightful. "I started and lost three businesses because I didn't know how to hire the right people. It was very costly and demoralizing."

As an entrepreneur and business owner, he was not alone in his confusion about how to select the right people.

Cost of a Bad Hire, Job Transfer, or Job Promotion

When you have a good basic estimate of what it costs every time you select the right person for the wrong job OR put the wrong person in the right job, you can easily cost justify using ATS (applicant tracking system), assessments, and a third-party vendor for due diligence.

Using the right processes and tools will result in great hires, improve retention, and increase your ability to transfer or promote the right people. Your customers will be happier too.

A Simple Hiring Calculation

Use annual payroll or individual employee cost and multiply by 35%.*

$250,000 (annual payroll) x .35 = $87,500 cost for payroll and benefits for the year

> *Since this percentage can vary from company to company based on geography, industry, and other factors, check with your professional association for your exact percentage, or calculate your own by designing a hiring calculator for your company.

Design a Hiring Calculator for Your Company

For a full review of hiring costs specific to your company, set up an Excel spreadsheet OR conduct an online search for a hiring mistake calculator.

The following are recommended items to get you started. Include other tangible and intangible items important in your company.

COSTS FOR ADMINISTRATIVE AND INTERVIEW TIME

- Acquire business cards or posters designed to attract qualified applicants.

- Set up ATS for each job posting.

- Review applications.

- Set up and conduct interviews (individual and team).

- Follow-up with applicants to answer questions, job offer letter, and negotiate.

- Process and review of assessment results.

- Create and update job match or benchmarks for assessments.

COST FOR RECRUITMENT AND SELECTION

- Write, distribute, and post job ads.

- Estimate relocation costs.

- Determine recruitment fees: use of third-party agency to find employees.

- Estimate cost of background checks, employment & education verification, reference checks (either cost of the person conducting these, or cost of a third-party vendor).

- Consider costs of assessments and skills testing tools.

- Include the annual cost for ATS website.

COST OF WAGES DURING "LEARNING CURVE"

- *Annual compensation of new employee.

- *Annual compensation of trainer(s)
  or supervisor(s).
  *Adjust the cost of these items by percentage of
  work not being completed: then, multiply by
  the number of days or months training is being
  provided.

COSTS FOR ACCOUNTING AND PAYROLL

- Set up new employee on payroll, including
  benefit enrollment and communication
  of options.

- Determine the cost of benefits and compensation.

- Estimate the cost of workers' compensation,
  unemployment, social security, and other
  mandated costs.

COST FOR OFFICE, REMOTE, AND EQUIPMENT

- Computer and other technology items:
  phone, printer, scanner, and software.

- Connections for remote employees.

- Office furniture for on-site employees.

- Safety equipment, vehicles, and uniforms.

- Cost of a trainer on the use of these items.

COSTS FOR EMPLOYEE ORIENTATION AND ONBOARDING

- Set up of program content, materials, and videos.

- Creation and delivery of programs (including hourly or daily cost of new employee attending).

- Cost of internal or outside trainer.

Notes ...

4

Two Key Questions That Must Be Answered for Each Open Position

---

Who are you looking for? **What** skills does the person need to be successful in the job?

While these questions may seem obvious, too often hiring bosses don't spend enough time (if any) answering them. Or they hire infrequently and they just want someone to do the job the way it's always been done as fast as possible.

This is where you need to get real about who and what you need. **Make your own list.** Then, brainstorm the required competencies for the position with key staff members. Remember, your business requirements and the economy can change frequently.

Ask and brainstorm:

- What actual qualities are required?

- What does the right candidate need to accomplish in the first 30-60-90-180 days?

- What job fit assessment is best to see the "whole person?"

Example: If you're seeking someone who can sell, should the salesperson also be able to generate leads, present, and close? Additionally, does this person need to provide exceptional customer care? (Different companies have different expectations from their successful salespeople.) Use a qualified job fit assessment to complement your interviews since these provide objective and consistent data to see the "whole person." (See Chapter 9: Use the Right Assessments and Skill Tests.)

Remember, during the interview, candidates will strive to look and speak their best. Make sure you are looking below the surface of experience, education, and other credentials to clearly understand if the person:

- Can do the job?
- Will do the job?
- Can do the job successfully here?

Notes ...

Notes ...

5

Create a Job Description

The primary purpose of a job description is to communicate the purpose of each job and the skills, education/training, and expectations required to do it successfully.

Now, it's time to write down the key job responsibilities or job specs to get everyone on the same page (boss, key employees, and new employees). While these do not need to be formal, they do need to meet certain employment guidelines.

Purpose of a Job Description

- "A job description is a useful, plain-language tool that explains the tasks, duties, functions, and responsibilities of a position.

- They can be used for a variety of reasons, such as determining salary levels, conducting performance reviews, clarifying missions, establishing titles and pay grades, and creating reasonable accommodation controls, as well as being a tool for recruiting.

- Job descriptions are useful in career planning, offering training exercises and establishing legal requirements for compliance purposes."[6]

A well-designed strategic selection system includes good job descriptions. They clarify job requirements for both the employee and the boss. They are a must!

When these requirements are written down in a job description format, you will speak differently and be consistent in what you are saying. Top performers are job and employer savvy. They listen for consistency. When you are consistent, you will attract more candidates and they are more likely to accept your job offers.

Conduct an online search for "job description template." There will be a variety of formats to choose from. Remember, pick the one that will work in your company for ALL positions! (Makes selection for hiring, job transfers, and job promotions much easier if everyone in your company is using the same template. Improves legal defensibility too.)

Getting Back to Basics

To get started, write down key job responsibilities. Remember, focus on the job and not on a particular person doing the job.

Answer the five Ws. (The "how" will be answered later in this book.)

1. **W**hy do you need the position?

2. **W**ho do you need?

3. **W**hat are the primary job responsibilities and expectations?

4. **W**hen does the new hire need to be fully competent in his/her work? (See Chapter 6: Create a 180-Day Success Plan.)

5. **W**here will the person be located?

Brainstorm with key employees to see what you've missed. Then, add the key job competencies required.

Example: Competencies for a project manager include: team building, resolving conflicts, and managing ROI for projects.

Note: Qualified job fit assessments provide benchmarking and can provide additional insights for true competencies required for job success.

Often Overlooked DO's and DON'Ts

Do's	Don'ts
Use easy to understand job titles.	*Catchy, cute or faddish titles that have no meaning to anyone outside of your company and can be embarrassing to explain. Also, fancy or long titles mean very little to most people.
Keep it simple and smart.	Long and wordy job descriptions are rarely read and rarely understood. Average reading level is 5th or 6th grade.
Focus on key responsibilities.	Listing every work responsibility and task (which can change frequently) is boring.
Encourage current employees to give input.	Writing descriptions for your employees when you've not worked in the position creates confusion.
Make it generic by removing biases.	Fail to update regularly.

Do's	Don'ts
Review before interviews.	Winging it and thinking you'll remember will cause candidates to disregard your job and company. Candidates are seeking consistency.

*Part of the attraction of the job is the status the job title provides to the successful incumbent. Have job titles match industry standards since incumbents want to share their new job title with pride. Some applicants have been known to decline positions due to unusual or poorly thought-out job titles!

Notes ...

6

Create a 180-Day Success Plan

A well written 180-Day Success Plan provides a clear road map for new job success.

This is in addition to the job description and is completed after the job description has been written. It provides a game plan for the boss and new incumbent with metrics, expectations, and milestones to ensure everyone is on the same page from day one. Search online for template, "180-Day Success Plan" to get you started.

The clearer you are about what you need the person to achieve, the more likely the new person will succeed in the job. The 180-Day Success Plan goes beyond the job description and gets everyone on the same page on "how" the newly selected person can learn about the job responsibilities and clarify the training and employee onboarding required to understand the company and expectations.

Remember, keep it simple and doable. I have seen well-designed plans help new people in new positions feel confident and comfortable. And, I've seen that when a boss expects too much too soon, the person feels like a failure and leaves quickly or stays with a negative attitude.

Spending time writing a game plan makes it easier to find the right person. During the interview, you will have clarity about the type of person you need and how to help him/her succeed.

This boosts your confidence and portrays you as a great (future) boss! (It's one of the critical traits top performers are seeking in their next opportunity: confident bosses who are clear about what they need and want and who have the know-how to develop them for success in their careers.)

Key factors:

- A well thought-out plan gets everyone on the same page.
- Improves the selection process.
- Focuses on key results required and how to achieve them.
- Includes specialized training, meeting with key employees and clients, and metrics to gauge success (e.g., number of network meetings for salespeople).
- This information should be shared with your final candidates.

Critical! If there is any hesitancy or unwillingness on the part of the job candidate to buy into any part of the job description or the 180-Day Plan, address it now! The concerns won't go away soon ... if ever.

Example: Diversity training required for all managers may be something a new manager shies away from citing s/he'd already done it. Remember, every company has its own workplace culture and what may be appropriate in one company may have a "no tolerance" policy in your company. This concern can be a red flag that must be addressed before the job offer!

Then, review the 180-Day Success Plan on the employee's first day in new job. You will find some new hires will have forgotten it or did not take you seriously. Again, address any hesitancies or problems now! These elephants can disappear when the right conversations occur.

Now, have each person design a specific action plan on how s/he will accomplish these "successes." Review immediately to ensure both of you are on the same page and fill in any missing details and certain people to meet first.

Set up a structure to review the results both weekly and at the end of each 30-day period. This keeps them, and you, focused on what is needed for their success, customer satisfaction, and the company's bottom line. If someone is about to or has already gone off-track, it's imperative you get them back on track now. If you wait or overlook the issue, you'll lose the employee and/or other top talent and great customers!

John, a sales manager for a $10M consumer product company, needed someone to open a new market for his company. Because he was immediately impressed by Teri's great interview skills and self-confidence in her abilities, he fast tracked her through the company's due diligence process without conducting a full interview or completing a qualified job fit assessment. Also, he failed to create a 180-Day Success Plan, citing he was too busy.

But Teri was not the same confident person when she arrived on day one. She felt lost and hesitant about what to do. John was often too busy putting out customer fires to guide her. When she asked about the sales training promised during the interview, John shook his head, not remembering his promise. He replied, "You really won't need it if you do what I tell you to do." (She'd previously been an internal customer service rep and left that job to work for John.) Teri was fired three months later.

Later that day, Scott, John's VP, reminded him of his responsibility to ensure his sales team had the required competencies, skills, and training before hiring, transferring, or promoting anyone.

John replied, "I thought I would train, coach, and motivate her to be a success. As you know, our customers' demands keep me busy."

Scott shook his head before replying, "When you have the right people in the right jobs, customer demands lessen! It's why we spent time creating a strategic selection system. When followed, it works! You need to follow it, or you will be the one looking for a new job."

If John had followed his company's strategic selection system and written a 180-Day Success Plan, Teri would not have been hired for this sales position, but she might have been selected for an inside sales position. Instead, she has a bitter experience to share with others about the company.

This happens all too often and is avoidable! Don't let it happen to you!

Notes ...

7

Select the Right
Applicant Tracking System (ATS)
and Learn How to Use It

The right Applicant Tracking System (ATS) for your company is a must today! It can handle your recruitment and hiring process: speed up managing candidates, posting jobs, and making job offers. And ATS can keep all activities in one place.

Managed correctly, it saves you hundreds of hours and thousands of dollars when vetting candidates and may include other time-savers. ATS ...

- Provides a systematic data collection point and allows recruiters to weed out those without the qualifications required.

- Automates replies to all applicants thanking them for their interest.

- Provides the ability to send out requests for additional information (e.g., completion of assessments or skills tests).

- May offer the ability to push to job boards, reducing time spent posting job ads.

Work with your provider to ensure the ATS is set up properly, all automated processes are working, and it's an easy system for job candidates to use and understand.

Employers of any size can look very impressive to job candidates when using a well-designed ATS. Those companies that still request resumes via email or mail are unattractive to top talent.

If you're using the right ATS and writing great job ads, it will attract qualified candidates regardless of the economy. Many times, the job postings or job ads will be the applicant's first introduction to your company. (See Chapter 8: Attract Qualified Job Candidates with Job Ads and Job Postings.)

If you need to expand your reach to increase the number and/or quality of candidates, the right ATS will allow you to sort and manage them effectively.

The key for success? The ATS process needs to be **easy and fast to use from the perspective of the job applicants.** You need to capture them now! If frustrated, most applicants will not return to the job ad, even with the best of intentions.

- Provide a short, attractive, and easy to read job posting with specific requirements.

- Ask Prescreening Questions to determine basic qualifications.

- Ask for contact information: phone, mobile, and email.

- Provide full employment application if there is an interest. (Reason explained later in this chapter.)

- Make it user-friendly. This means that in one or two clicks the job candidates go from the job posting directly to the application site to read about the job and apply. Otherwise, they become fearful of falling prey to spam! This is true when using QR Codes too.

- Ensure systems are working and the contact person is responsive. Qualified job applicants will by-pass any employer (regardless of size and reputation) because their systems didn't work or contact person didn't respond.

Select the Right ATS for Your Company

Remember, these systems are not all created alike. Be clear what you want, need, and desire before selecting one. As always, "test drive" it first … just like when purchasing a new vehicle!

I would recommend you talk with three (not more) vendors and do a comparison. One of the "vendors" may be your own internal tech team.

Here's a suggested checklist of questions to be asked and answered:

- Does the system post to job boards or other job sites?

- If yes, what are they? Can the list be expanded? Is there an additional cost?

- Is it easy to use from company and job applicant experiences?

- Can the company and job applicant easily use a mobile phone or tablet to access and complete the form(s)?

- Will the system automatically send a "thank you" email to let the applicant know his/her information was received?

- Will the system allow you to interact with candidates to obtain additional information or set automatic requests for: completion of assessments, answering Prescreening Questions, or chatting with the recruiter.

- Does the system contain the prewritten application form, job posting format, applicant request for additional information, and other pertinent information? Can these be easily modified to fit the company's needs?

- Are hiring managers or recruiters notified when an application is completed?

- Does the site prevent resumes from being "blasted" to the company without filling out the basic required information?

- Can you use keyword searches (e.g., experience, certifications, education)?

- Will it notify interested applicants of future positions? A good applicant may not be qualified for or interested in the position you are recruiting for today. Keep candidates interested in your company with notifications of future opportunities (with their permission).

- Can you collect Equal Employment Opportunity (EEO) or other required information? Tracking may be required if you have any government contracts or are a subcontractor for federal, state, county, and city contracts.

- Is there a human verification used to reduce spam? Make this process easy!

- Usernames and passwords often are not remembered! How does the site handle these concerns?

- Does the system provide reminders to the hiring manager or recruiter to follow-up and honor promises made to interviewees going past the first interview? Remember, lack of communication is a common complaint by candidates. *Don't ever forget!* These applicants may become future clients, vendors, or decision makers! It pays to take the time to send a letter or email, even if it is an automated one.

- What is the monthly or annual cost for set up and maintenance of the ATS site?

Finally, take the time to ensure that the site you select, the jobs you post, and the application procedures are working successfully by polling users. If potential applicants get frustrated with your online process, they'll move on to another employer. Remember, your goal is to showcase your company as a great employer! It starts with a well-designed ATS.

Create Prescreening Questions

This is a great time-saver and way to determine if an applicant has the basic must-have skills or required experiences and education. Keep it to no more than five questions or you risk losing great candidates.

Be sure to ask the right questions:

- Focus on required skills, education, or job experiences and job results.

- Answers can be open-ended, yes or no, or multiple choice.

- Questions must be specific and critical to success. Example: Have you ever been a manager of 20+ employees? Why were you successful as a manager?
- Do not ask personal questions.
- Analysis of answers can uncover qualified applicants who were overlooked when using keyword searches.

One Example: A property management company seeking a property manager might ask:

- What are the largest number of units and size of properties that you have managed?
- What has been your average occupancy rate?
- What is an acceptable delinquency rate for a property?

Second Example: A manufacturing company seeking an accountant might ask:

- Do you have a CPA designation? If yes, year and where obtained?
- What type of accounting software have you used?
- How many years of experience have you had with A/R and A/P and Payroll?

Why Employers Should Require That a Full Application Be Completed

Application forms play an important role in the selection process. They give the hiring manager initial information about an applicant. It's best to review application forms prior to the interview.

Also, application forms are considered a legal document.

To encourage busy or hesitant applicants to apply, you may request basic information along with Prescreening Questions. If there is further interest from the company, require full completion of the application form. Do not allow the applicant to say, "See Resume."

By collecting the full application and resume, along with any objective data that can be gathered prior to the job offer, you can reduce the time spent trying to second-guess what is true and what is not.

- Applications are legal documents signed by the applicant attesting that s/he has the skills, experience, and education as submitted.

- The form should be easy to read and complete and can only ask job related questions.

- Do NOT ask about age, gender, ethnicity, marital status, or family of origin. These are prohibited!

- Never rely solely on information contained in resumes. Remember, resumes are marketing materials.

- To streamline process, have the full application completed after an initial review of information provided on ATS or after the Phone Screen Interview (See Chapter 10). This increases the probability of applicants being qualified prior to spending time conducting a full interview.

Important Note About Resumes: Why Companies Should Not Rely Solely on Them

On average, 85 percent of resumes contain lies or inaccuracies.[7]

Many applicants embellish their career history with degrees never earned, exaggerated salaries, questionable job duties and results, additional years of employment, and names of employers pulled from "thin air." Even worse, you don't know which parts may be lies!

All too often, a resume is the only document collected in response to job postings. If there is no additional information requested or reviewed, this dramatically increases your time spent talking with candidates that don't meet the requirements for the position and decreases the likelihood of finding top performers. (On average, less than six seconds is spent when skimming a resume.)

A resume:

- Is written as a sales promotion and will contain inaccuracies, incorrect dates of employment, and nonexistent companies and/or education degrees.

- Makes objective data collection impossible since actual metrics will be missing (e.g., actual dates of employment, actual sales results, quality of skills).

Remember, the purpose of a well-designed strategic selection system is to collect enough of the right objective data on a consistent basis so you can improve how you hire, transfer, and/or promote amazing employees!

Keep Job Applicants Engaged

After a job candidate has indicated an interest in a position(s), provide the following to keep the person interested in working for your company.

- Provide a short video thanking the job candidate for applying.

- Share what to expect during the interview process if selected, providing tips and links to help the person prepare.

- Share short clips about the company's products and services. Keep in mind that it is probably the first time the person has heard of your company.

- Provide short on-point written material about the company's goals, locations, and fun facts. (Remember, on average, people read at a 5th or 6th grade level.)

Notes …

8

Attract Qualified
Job Candidates with Job Ads
and Job Postings

Now that you've selected and set up your ATS and written your job description and 180-Day Success Plan, you're ready to post job ads!

The best way to attract qualified job candidates is with well-written job ads. These need to be short and to-the-point since job seekers will not read long (or boring) job postings.

Candidates are cautious about whether or not to leap from their current employer or job because, in their current position, they understand the work responsibilities, department or company culture, and boss and customer expectations (even if they don't like them). Most refuse to reach out to employers they have not heard of or who have poor reputations on job boards.

For many, your job ad or posting is the applicant's first exposure to your company!

It needs to:

- Have job appeal with an attention-grabbing title and opening line.

- Focus on job applicants' interests (e.g., no experience required; will provide training while being paid).

- List the key skills required and opportunities for remote work, promotion, bonuses, etc.

- Be short, easy-to-read, and to-the-point. (Remember, the average reading level is 5th or 6th grade.)

- Have a direct link. (SEE URL or QR Code Link Etiquette on next page.)

- Provide an acknowledgment that the application was received.

- Have been written by your marketing or salespeople. They are in the best position to sell your company and the opportunities available to potential employees.

Remember, long ads with long lists of qualifications are rarely read! If you must post them, provide a link to a separate page next to the link for "Apply for Job."

URL or QR Code Link Etiquette

- The link must take applicants directly to the modified or full application.

- Do not send them to a general listing of all open positions, unless the posting is for general job openings.

- Links do break so test them each time they are posted.

- If the position has been filled or the opening has expired, delete your post. But post a short note thanking them for their interest if by chance they use an outdated link. Then, provide a different link that takes them directly to the general job posting site. Keep in mind, some job board sites will post expired job postings.

- Use a link that is easy to read if they need to write it down or take a picture. Use lower- and upper-case letters or actual words to make it easier to read.

- Keep the link short and use a link shortener if necessary.

Writing Job Ads and Postings That Attract Better Candidates

Job ads are the #1 method to attract qualified job candidates.

Here are four key factors to get your job ads noticed:

1. The job ad title is most important.

Candidates quickly skim online and rarely review ads later. It's why titles that are misleading, boring, or jargony are overlooked. It's also why companies receive many nonqualified applications.

Examples to Avoid:

- Strategic Initiatives Coordinator (This title is too jargony. The company is looking for an accounts manager.)

- Independent Contractors Needed – $$$ Sign-On Bonus $$ (In this case, the company needs drivers, but the headline is too vague.)

- Help Wanted (Help for what? Be more specific, e.g., manager of payroll department.)

Improved Examples:

- Previous moving experience NOT REQUIRED and training provided (Hint: Many positions require advanced **training.**)

- Build your career as a financial analyst – plenty of growth potential (Hint: People want to **advance** in their careers.)

2. Job ad content needs to be concise and provide attractive reasons to apply.

- Use bullet points.

- Provide the must-have qualifications to be considered.

- Keep the list short and get real about the requirements: many job candidates will not read a long list believing they won't be able to meet all requirements listed.

- Include job title. (See Chapter 5: Create a Job Description.)

- Do NOT include a long summation about the company. Instead provide one or two short sentences about the company. Remember, if you send them to the company's website, they usually will not come back to the job posting or ATS.

3. Qualified job candidates will apply to well-written job ads that address their concerns.

Example of areas to emphasize:

- **Poll your employees and/or job applicants.** Find out their top concerns and address them.

- **Include company name, address and map:**
  Blind ads do not attract top talent. Applicants
  want jobs close to home or with the ability to
  work remotely. So, include the company's
  address and a map of the location.

- **Provide expectations for work hours, travel,
  benefits, and pay:** short bullet points that
  share hours, pay rate, training requirements,
  remote or hybrid work available, flexible
  hours, benefits, and team/individual bonuses.

4. **A quick and easy mobile application process
   is required.** Provide prominent links to the
   company's applicant tracking system.

Additional Resources for Job Ads and Postings

Do you need to expand your resources to find well-qualified
job candidates?

- Here's a simple test to determine whether you
  need to find new resources:

  Review the W-2s issued for the two previous years.
  Compare the number of W-2s with the number of
  employees you presently have. How much staff
  change is revealed? The bigger the discrepancy,
  the more you will want to brainstorm on how to
  find and locate untapped groups of potential
  employees.

Utilizing new sources can help you find hidden talent and people who may be unaware of you as a potential employer.

EMPLOYEE REFERRALS

This is often an untapped resource! Provide incentives for current employees to provide referrals. You will be rewarded with the best of all possible recruiting payoffs: more amazing employees.

- When announcing these job opportunities to your employees, provide them with the direct link to a specific job or the general postings using the ATS link.

- Remember, it's critical that everyone apply for the job(s) using the same ATS. It keeps all applications in one place and makes it easier for you to review the data, now and in the future. It also provides documentation if your company is ever audited by the Department of Labor (DOL) or is handling any related litigation.

- Develop a simple business card with the URL and/or QR Code link listed for the general ATS site, or provide the links on the back of business cards. If possible, include a QR code (conduct online search for "QR code" details). These are handy for posters or people adept with using their phones.

- Encourage your employees to hand out posters and cards, leaving them at community or public sites, or by posting them on approved bulletin boards.

- Include the same information in the signature line for all emails being sent out from your company.

OTHER COMPANY CONTACTS

Every business will naturally have local networks to tap into.

- Business contacts (clients, vendors, suppliers, professional and trade associations).

- Social groups (bowling leagues, religious groups, youth groups, condominium and neighborhood associations, senior and refugee centers, parent-teacher associations).

GOVERNMENT

Search the internet, social media sites and newspapers, and network with local employers to find the most effective government resources. For example, contact unemployment offices, community alliances, veteran outreach, and other similar offices for job seekers in your area.

NOT-FOR-PROFIT ORGANIZATIONS

Contact not-for-profit organizations that represent or assist underserved populations.

- Groups for people with disabilities, low-income support centers, women's resource centers, veterans' associations, refugee community groups, religious centers, and similar organizations.

- Many provide social media sites and online communities where you can post on their "job seeker" boards.

- Don't forget to include appropriate hashtags (#) to increase online interest in your jobs (e.g., #hiring #jobseekers #IT).

FOR-PROFIT CORPORATIONS

- Invest time talking with groups that provide outplacement services for companies.

- Consider traditional staffing and professional contractor agencies. Insist they use your strategic selection system to ensure job fit and a safe workplace with a focus on quality.

- Take advantage of for-profit companies that have announced cutbacks and contact them. Their loss can be your gain!

ADVERTISING

This is probably the most common and easiest form of recruitment. Don't forget to include your ATS link!

- The classic "want ad" can be posted in community and association newsletters and on cable TV or the company's website. Use direct mail pieces, chamber of commerce mailings to their members, religious publications, doorknob hangers, lawn and light pole signs. The lists are endless.

- Some companies include job opportunities with their invoices and sales receipts.

- Host a company open house, a job fair, or fund an event.

- Don't forget to post ads on social media and send out special invites via email or mail.

RELATIONSHIPS WITH LOCAL SCHOOLS

- Have managers and up-and-coming leaders within your company speak at secondary schools, community colleges, technical and trade schools, and universities.

- Place job postings in career centers, school newspapers, college dorms, or their intranet sites for current students and graduates.

- Volunteer at educational events and competitions, such as speaking contests, science fairs, or sports events.

- Hire interns and consider them for future opportunities within your organization.

- Don't forget! Send or take and distribute the ATS business cards and posters!

TARGETED INTRODUCTIONS

- Contact potential candidates via emails or through professional/personal connections. These avenues can help you uncover qualified people. Potential candidates can be found on many social media sites, in trade or professional membership rosters, or through other venues.

- Utilize diplomacy when reaching out to these contacts via phone, letters, or emails.

- Remain easily accessible and responsive via phone, emails, face-to-face meetings, or a video conferencing platform.

- Remember, you initiated the contact. Failure to follow-up can create a poor reputation for your company and damage future sales when you are not responsive.

- After completing the initial conversations with referred job candidates, request the candidates apply through your ATS. They need to be vetted before you can proceed, just like any other candidate.

Notes ...

Notes ...

9

Use the Right Assessments and Skill Tests

As one business owner recently stated, "If it weren't for assessments, I would hire the way I always do and get the same bad results!" — President, Engineering Company

To improve your retention, revenues, and results, select qualified job fit and core value assessments, and quality skill tests. When used as designed, they will dramatically improve getting the right person in the right job!

The quality of these assessments and skill tests lets job candidates and internal employees know you are committed to putting the right person in the right job. These should also be used for internal job transfers and job promotions since these are your most costly, often unrecognized mistakes.

Using qualified assessments and skill tests can greatly enhance any company's selection process and lead to people working in new jobs that they enjoy and where they become amazing employees!

Many applicants have been well trained on how to be interviewed and how to answer frequently asked questions. They know how to say the right things, make promises you want to hear, and provide great work samples. These conversations do not accurately predict what the person can and may do on the job in your company.

High-quality assessment tools can provide you with information that most job candidates won't tell you, and may not themselves realize.

Job Candidates Are Like Pyramids

You usually only see 10% of the tip of the pyramid (past work experiences, school records, and other activities) and then you make many assumptions as to their suitability for the job.

People are like Pyramids buried in the sand.
90% of the whole person is below the surface.

10% – Education, Skills, and Experience is good, but limited information.
Determined from resumes, interviews, references

90% – The Whole Person
Obtained from qualified assessments: thinking styles, core behaviors, core values, occupational interests

- You can't see the other 90 percent (thinking styles, core behaviors, occupational interests/motivations, honesty/integrity) that determine actual success in the job. (Can they do the job? Will they do the job? Can they do the job successfully here?)

The purpose of using qualified job fit and core value assessments and of testing for job skills is to get real about each applicant's fit with the job responsibilities.

Types of assessment tools that provide good objective information to predict a candidate's success on the job:

- Thinking Style (Can they do the job?)
- Interests/Motivations (Will they do the job?)
- Behavioral Traits (Can they do the job here?)
- Job Matching (Will they fit successfully in the position?)
- Core Values (Are they reliable? Do they have acceptable integrity and work ethic?)
- Skills (Do they have the proficiency or dexterity required?) Note: Use skill testing regardless of certifications and education.

Qualified assessments have several things in common:

- Provide highest level of valid and reliable information due to thorough research.

- Predict success in a specific job.

- Provide a technical manual for your review.

- Verify or contradict your "gut/intuition."

- Prevent "biases" from getting in the way.

- Are tested to be nondiscriminatory.

- Help you meet all federal, state, and local statutes. (For international candidates, check with that country's requirements.)

- Validate the quality of information the candidate is providing: Is it accurate, or what they think you want, or what they wish they were … or a mix of all three?

- Used as directed, they work!

To find resources for these assessment products, go online and type in "assessments" or "skill testing." These searches can get you started in finding the right tool for your use.

To Get Started, Review the Technical Manual

To ensure each assessment tool is valid and reliable for preemployment and selection purposes, request a technical manual from the publisher or vendor for the assessment product.

A technical manual documents the research and development required to meet Department of Labor (DOL) (*Testing and Assessment: An Employer's Guide to Good Practices*), Equal Employment Opportunity (EEO), Americans with Disability Act (ADA), and other requirements for the assessment to be used for pre-employment and selection purposes. It helps you determine if the assessment meets minimum validity and reliability requirements[8] for use in your specific employment location(s).

Beware: some vendors may provide a letter from their attorney stating the assessment meets all applicable laws for hiring and selection purposes. That letter protects them, not you. Do your homework!

These questions are not inclusive when deciding to use a particular assessment. They are suggestions to get you started.

- Does it assess job-related skills?

- Does it meet all legal requirements for your work locations?

- Does it have recent validity and reliability tests?

- Does it provide predictive validity, high enough to meet DOL standards?

- What are the sample sizes and makeup for those tests (e.g., Is it validated with a large sample of working people, or a small sample of college sophomores)?

- Is it appropriate for preemployment selection and hiring purposes?

- Are you planning to use it for its intended purpose?

Caution: Just because an assessment is being used for training or coaching purposes and shows differences in people, does not mean that it can be used for preemployment and selection purposes. Not only is using the right assessment of legal importance, but it also ensures that you are using tools that actually have the validity and reliability required to measure the person accurately and objectively.

Purpose of Reliability vs. Validity and Why It's Critical

Review the reliability and validity scores in the product's technical manual. It is important to understand the differences between reliability and validity.

- Validity tells you if an assessment measures what it purports to measure.

- Predictive Validity tells you if it will predict success on the job.

- Reliability will tell you how trustworthy a score on that test will be over time. You cannot predict behavior on the job from a test score unless you are sure that the test is reliable. The reliability of a test is indicated by the reliability coefficient. It is denoted by the letter "r," and is expressed as a number ranging between 0 and 1.00.

These numbers matter! The higher the coefficient (aka number) and sample size (number of people being tested), the better the quality of the assessment.

- A product with low validity and reliability numbers will not help improve your selection process regardless of the sample size.

- A product with high validity and reliability numbers with small sample sizes will not help improve your selection process.

- To make the biggest difference in your selection process, use assessments that have the highest validity and reliability numbers with large sample sizes.

Use of Cut Offs with Assessments and Skill Testing

These tools should only account for about one-third of the selection decision. However, you may use cut offs when following the Department of Labor guidelines.

- A cut off is a determining factor that the applicant must meet in order to be further considered for the job. If you use cut offs, be sure these are used consistently, objectively, and meet any legal requirements. Include the conditions in your strategic selection system. Example, if you are using a skill test and require a score of 80 or higher, you would no longer consider applicants that fall below a score of 80.

Remember, top performers have become savvier about legally qualified assessments. Be sure to only use qualified tools as part of the selection process: preemployment, job transfer, and promotion.

Skill Testing

Skill testing goes beyond the "certificate" or "license" or "degree" and discerns the depth of individuals' knowledge and experience. It can be used to eliminate a candidate or to identify the level of training that will need to be provided.

Remember, some skills can be developed on the job. Have candidates complete job skill tests to determine their level of proficiency and any future training required. Job fit assessments can determine if they will have the interest to improve these skills and how they will do it.

Be wary! It's a myth that a high level of job skills equates to good job fit. Only use reliable and valid job fit assessments to provide consistent and objective measures.

Example: Many tradespeople claim to understand "maintenance." The problem is, even with certificates and licensing, it doesn't mean they have the knowledge required for your business. I've seen this expensive lesson happen too often and the problem ignored until there was a crisis (e.g., HVAC stopped working in subzero temps in an apartment complex and took several days to get repaired; or the pool remained closed during the summer at a popular resort).

Core Value Assessments

Qualified core value assessments (aka honesty/integrity) provide direct admission information. Candidates are requested to admit whether they have taken item(s), data, and/or money, their attitude toward bosses, their willingness to show up for work, how well they follow rules, their personal use of the internet on company time, and so on.

Since many applicants embellish the truth or lie, it's critical to the safety and well-being of the workplace to discover anything not known readily or that will fail to show up in a public record. Remember, most employers do not prosecute an employee for theft or share information about the person's poor work habits.

Studies have shown that job candidates will admit things to a computer that they would never admit to an interviewer!

While background checks may help you learn what a candidate has done in the past, core value assessments can predict what they might do in the future.

Keep in mind, theft from employees today can add up to hundreds of thousands of dollars annually, per employee, from all levels of employees. White-collar crime involving money, data, and proprietary information is the fastest growing crime in corporate America.

When used as part of the recruiting process, qualified core value assessment will dissuade those who have something to hide or are not really interested in your company. Refer to local, state, and federal statutes, and the vendor guidelines and technical manual for the assessments for regulations on how and when you can use core value assessments.

Job Fit Assessments

Remember, you hire for perceived job skills. You fire for poor job fit.

Good job fit is the #1 predictor of job satisfaction, retention, and productivity.[9] Satisfied employees reduce miscommunication and team conflict, while meeting and exceeding required results for customers and the company's bottom line. When you use a qualified job fit assessment, you can improve diversity, coach with effectiveness, and establish meaningful career paths for employees.

A qualified assessment allows us to see the whole person, including the 90 percent that is often camouflaged by resumes depicting a person's education, skills and job experience, and further hidden by the quality of someone's interview skills.

Job Fit and Job Matching

It's important to establish clarity as to the traits that will make for a successful job fit. This is accomplished by creating job matching.

Job fit or job matching is critical to ensuring success for the person being selected for a position. These particular traits may vary per company, geography, position, and managerial style. One way to determine job matching criteria is using the assessment with current employees. An added benefit is that this is also a great way to provide diversity training and leadership development for your current employees too. It helps team members appreciate differences in each other. Refer to the vendor and technical manual for other recommendations to create job matching patterns.

Using these job matching patterns can also facilitate selection and coaching reports. It's recommended that you use them as guides when asking behavioral interview questions. Chapters 13 and 14 cover more about interviewing guidelines.

Time-Saver When Using Assessments and Skill Testing: Set up your ATS to remind applicants to complete any assessments or skill testing. Check with the assessment/test vendor and technical manual to determine when and how these can be used before the job offer.

A young man was given a great opportunity to become a team leader. His employer used their strategic selection system before promoting him. While they knew there were areas for him to develop on the job, they wanted to be sure of his true interest and ability to grow into these new job duties. The job fit assessment helped to craft a leadership development plan to guide him for success.

Even if they want the job, applicants do not want to end up as a future hiring mistake. Remember, it's critical to have clear awareness about the job candidate's current abilities and realistic expectations of where to focus in order to develop the person for success. Otherwise, it'll cost you a lot of time, money, top talent, and great customers. (No one wants to retrain your selection misfits.)

Notes ...

10

Phone Screen Interview Questions, Full Interview Questions, and Reference Check Questions

---

Remember to focus on job-related questions.

Stay away from those questions that are **not appropriate** to ask.

These include:

- Personal (e.g., age, race, marital status, family history)

- Infer behavioral characteristics (e.g., most recent book read or movie seen, favorite sport, color preferences)

The following set of questions will get you started in designing your own company's process.

Remember:

- The same questions must be asked of all job candidates being interviewed for a particular position.

- Have the phone, in-person, and reference check questions readily accessible to all hiring managers. The responses to the questions will facilitate the hiring manager's task of choosing the candidate best suited for the open position.

- Don't forget to provide procedures along with the strategic selection system for how and when to use each set of questions to conduct interviews and reference checks.

Phone Screen Interview Questions

This is a huge time saver when used effectively. In Chapter 13, there are recommendations on how to get the most out of this process.

- Date & Time:
- Name of Applicant:
- Phone number:
- Email address:
- Name of Interviewer:
- Has resume been reviewed?
  YES___ NO___ (If no, why not?)

- Review for <u>each</u> employer listed on the resume and application form:
  - Actual start and end dates of employment
  - Why did you leave?
- Tell me about yourself and your professional background.
- What are your salary expectations?
- What are you looking for in your next position?
- Why are you leaving your present position (if currently employed)?
- Why did you leave your former employer (if currently unemployed)?
- What type of work environment are you looking for?
- Have you ever worked remotely? If yes, what were the challenges?
- Have you ever managed others' work? If yes, what were the successes and failures? What do you believe were the causes for them? (Beware if there were no failures.)

Full Interview Questions

Make sure questions are job focused on what they've done, what they would like to do, and why. This creates a much better candidate experience since the questions are focused on them. In Chapter 14, there are recommendations on how to get the most out of this process.

Note: Use Drill Down Method. (See Chapter 12 to learn more about how to use to determine the levels of their skills and talents.)

- Tell me about your work experience in ...
  (Be very specific here. Have four to seven areas of importance to the open position written down.)

- Please share three of your strengths and why you believe they are strengths.

- Please share three areas for improvement or what might be considered weaknesses. Why are these important?

- Have you handled a job remotely full- or part-time? How did that work for you? What are the pros? What are the cons or biggest challenges?

- For supervisory, manager, director, or executive positions: How many people have you managed? What were your successes? What were your failures?

- Tell me about your most recent job-related mistake. What did you do to handle or resolve it?

- How would you describe your work habits?

- How do you handle "change" in your job or in the workplace? Can you give a recent example?

- Describe your leadership experience and how you feel that experience will benefit you in this job.

- If I were to talk with others, how would they describe you?
  - Coworkers?
  - Direct Reports?
  - Bosses?
  - Customers?

- Is there anything else you believe is important for us to know about you that we haven't covered?

- Do you have any questions? (Be wary if prospective employee doesn't have any questions. The person either didn't prepare or falsely believes s/he understands the job requirements.)

Reference Check Questions

(See Conduct Professional Reference Checks in Chapter 17.)

- Date & Time:
- Name of Applicant:
- Name of Reference:
- Reference's phone number:
- Reference's email:
- Completed by:

- How do you know the applicant? For how long?

- What was the applicant's job? Location?

- How does the applicant get along with others? Can you give specific examples?
  - Coworkers?
  - Customers?
  - Supervisors?

- How well did the applicant follow through on completing assignments? Timeliness? Quality? Please give one or two examples.

- Did the applicant take directions well?

- If the applicant worked remotely:
  - How well did he or she complete assignments?
  - Was most of the work done onsite, remote, or hybrid?

- Did the person show up for online calls or in-person meetings as required?

- If the applicant will supervise or manage people:
  - How well did he or she direct others' work?
  - What was the number of people managed and the type of positions?
  - Were these onsite, remote, or hybrid workers?
  - How long did the applicant manage these people?
  - What was his or her management style? How effective was it?

- How was the applicant's attendance and punctuality?

- Please share three of the applicant's strengths.

- Please share three areas for improvement or that might be considered weaknesses.

- If the applicant needs to make presentations:
  - Please evaluate the applicant's speaking skills in groups, meetings, presentations, etc.

- What were the applicant's major accomplishments on the job? Why were these achievements important?

- Would you rehire the applicant? Would you work for the applicant? Why or why not?

  I found this to be a very telling question to ask. It wasn't the "yes" or "no" that was insightful. Rather, it was the response to the follow-up question of "Why?"

- Do you know anyone else from whom we can get a reference?

Notes ...

Notes ...

Part 2

First and Second Sides of the Selection Triad: Interviews and Assessments

Remember, the interview is one-third of the selection decision and assessments are one-third of the selection decision!

11

Purpose of the Interview

Most companies rely on interviews as a decisive factor when selecting job candidates and making job offers. Yet, interviews alone only predict job success a tiny fraction of the time. We often overlook more important indicators that can ensure the person fits the job.

The interview should only account for one-third of the selection decision. Assessments equal another one-third, and due diligence is the final one-third of a well-designed strategic selection system.

The goal of any interview is to gather good, objective data on each person by asking the right questions and listening to his/her responses.

The key? Collect enough reliable and valid information prior to an interview to ensure that the person has what is required to succeed in the job. Then, use the interview process to validate. It saves time and money and keeps you focused on finding the right amazing employee.

The three primary questions that must be answered for any selection process (e.g., preemployment, job transfer, or job promotion) are:

- Can this candidate do the job?
- Will this candidate do the job?
- Can this candidate do the job successfully here?

These are easy to answer if you are prepared and use all three sides of the Selection Triad. Common interview challenges are included to help interviewers become mindful of inherent biases that can get in the way so they can avoid them. (See Common Interview Challenges in Chapter 12.)

Notes ...

Notes ...

12

Pointers for Successful Interviews

A good practice when selecting candidates for interviews:

- Prescreen 10 to 15 candidates.

- Conduct a Full Interview of five or six candidates.

- Select the final three candidates before making a job offer.

Trust your strategic selection system and follow it. Remember, selection is a process, not a one-time event!

- Turn off electronic devices and other distractions during interviews. When everyone does this, the interview is more productive and saves time.

- For virtual interviews, be sure everyone is visible on your monitor during 1:1 or group interviews. Everyone must stay on video, focused on the interview, and not multitasking!

- Have every person take his/her own notes.

- Start the interview by introducing yourself (20 seconds). If in a group, have each interviewer provide a 20-second intro. State name, title, and how this job impacts his/her area. For example, *"Today I am (or, we are) conducting the first set of interviews for XXX position. This interview will take approximately one hour. Have you scheduled this amount of time for our conversation?"* (If no, reschedule to ensure consistency in the interview process.)

- Stick with your structured interview format for each job. ALL candidates for a particular position need to be asked the same basic questions, regardless of gender, race, ethnicity, or other factors. Also, ask the same questions for candidates being considered for rehire, job transfer, promotion, and contractors or consultants wanting to be moved to full- or part-time employment. **Again, ask ALL job candidates the same basic questions.**

- Make sure all interview questions are focused on requirements for the job, and not questions to "infer" their personality (e.g., what's your favorite color?).

- The applicant is there to be interviewed. Ask open-ended questions to get the person talking. Then listen!

- Use Drill Down Method to ensure clarity about an interviewee's comments. (See page 122.)

- Ask the questions contained in assessment reports. A qualified assessment normally provides behaviorally based and legally reviewed interview questions. (Check with assessment vendor.)

- Write notes of promises made during the interview. Keep these with the interview and candidate notes.

- Don't spend time pitching or selling your company. The job candidate is not there to buy a product or service.

- At the end of the interview, *not the beginning,* share the information below. Remember KISS (**k**eep **i**t **s**imple and **s**mart). Here's why: *You want the job candidate to tell you who s/he really is ... not what s/he thinks you want to hear.*

  - Vision and mission of the company.

  - Job title and top three to five job responsibilities (do not negotiate now).

  - Quick overview of 180-Day Plan.

- **DO NOT** conduct salary and benefit negotiations until it's time to make a job offer.

- Share what happens next with selected candidates (e.g., future interviews with team members, reference and education verifications, job fit assessments).

Drill Down Method

This is a great method to get underneath the positive impression candidates hope to make.

- Process: Ask a question three times, being more specific each time, to get the facts.

- Provides you with clarification and eliminates guessing (often incorrectly) about the person's true ability and experience to do the job.

- Saves time and reduces making a bad hiring decision based on an assumption of the candidate's talent, skills, and job fit.

One not-for-profit organization was having a difficult time finding the right person for a particular position. The executive director admitted that he would only ask twice for clarification of an important question or statement. His rationale was that if he needed to ask more than that, he wouldn't have the patience to work with that applicant. Maybe. Maybe not. When you ask three times, being more specific each time, you get to the facts. It reveals a candidate's true competencies instead of glossing over pertinent details.

If you need to use this approach too often, it may be true that when the person is not forthcoming in his/her responses, s/he may not be the right person for the job.

Here are two examples using the Drill Down Method. The intention is to ask three questions to uncover the truth.

Example #1

Interviewer: Tell me about your Accounts Payable experience?

Response: I've done it.

Interviewer: Specifically, what have you done?

Response: Entered the data.

Interviewer: Then what did you do with the data?

Response: Gave it to my boss.

The interviewer now knows the applicant has little experience doing A/P for the level of work s/he needs done.

Example #2 (asking an hourly employee about starting work on time)

Interviewer: Are you normally right on time for work?

Response: Normally right on time ... but once in a while I may be late.

Interviewer: What does "once in a while" mean?

Response: Well ... my current supervisor ignores lateness.

Interviewer: How late is late?

Response: Maybe 15 minutes or so.

Interviewer: At this company, we start on time.
If you're normally late, we would have to suspend
you. Are you still interested in talking further?

Be Prepared! It's Critical to Well-Conducted Interviews

Preparing for the interview is as important as the interview itself.

Many employers admit that structured and behavioral-based interviews are important. But that knowledge makes no difference if you don't take the time to use a well-designed interview approach. The interview is where hiring bosses create a good or bad image of the company.

Use a Preparation Checklist for the Interview

✓ Review the Job Description (this may include talking with employees who work directly with or in that position).

✓ Review job requirements that are often overlooked (e.g., overtime, travel, actual work schedule and expectations, challenges of working remotely).

✓ Review 180-Day Success Plan. This will be shared with final candidates. It also serves as a reminder of the results you need the person in the position to achieve in order to succeed. Be sure to structure your interview questions accordingly.

✓ Determine a set of structured interview questions. Use open-ended questions that are customized to fit the specific position. (See Interview Questions in Chapter 10.)

✓ When setting up a team interview or selecting individuals to conduct interviews, keep the number to three to five. Provide them with an interview format and questions. Ensure they are trained in asking legally proper questions. Talk with them directly to ensure that any hidden agendas or self-interests (e.g., their own candidates, desire to hire for diversity) will not impede the interview. Sadly, conflicts do erupt at inappropriate times, leaving candidates with less than positive experiences (which they share with others).

✓ Review and look for any discrepancies when comparing the fully completed application form, Prescreening Questions, notes from previous interview(s), resume, assessments, and other test results. Make this information available, as appropriate, to the team of interviewers.

Example, do not share job fit or core value assessment results with future coworkers conducting interviews since they are contributors and not decision makers.

✓ Remember, to help prevent bias and ensure job requirements are being addressed, ask the same basic questions of each candidate.

✓ Ask additional questions as determined by each candidate's specific responses and when using Drill Down Method (See page 122.)

I've found that many times it can be the less than "ideal" looking and speaking candidate who may be the smartest and best fit for the job! It's the reason wise hiring managers have three top candidate finalists!

Here Are Common Interview Challenges before, during, and after the Interview

This information is provided to help interviewers become mindful of inherent interview biases.

• Managers hire, transfer, or promote the person who looks the part, talks the part, and uses the right jargon. Many managers are often dismayed to find out later that it was the wrong person for the right job. Or, the right person placed in the wrong job.

- Believe someone fits the job due to the job candidate's strong verbal skills. Although an individual is adept at telling interviewers what they want to hear and is very articulate, it does not mean person has the ability to do the job.

- Hire contractor or consultant as full- or part-time employee. The challenge is the person may behave differently as an employee, or the boss may unconsciously treat him/her differently.

- Transfer or promote a top performer to a different position does not mean the person will be a top performer in this other position. This is an expensive, unrecognized cost many companies face when the person lands in the wrong job and doesn't fit the work responsibilities.

- Failing to listen or to use Drill Down Method to ascertain true ability, interest, and willingness to do the whole job.

  Examples include:

  - Promotion to a position that requires managing numbers when the individual hired has no interest in financial matters.

  - Project management that requires developing team members when the person has no interest in managing people.

- Problem-solving flexibility needed to address sensitive customers' needs when the person chosen lacks diplomacy.

- Using a shortcut strategic selection system citing intuition or gut as the determining factor, which is often wrong.

- Falling prey to education bias, believing a higher education degree makes someone a top performer. Or believing a candidate that graduated from the same alma mater or an Ivy League school will make the person a better fit for the job. There is no objective relationship between where a person went to college and whether or not s/he has the interest or aptitude for the job!

- Demographic variables such as age, race, or gender (of both interviewer and interviewee) have been shown to influence interviewer judgments. Example: ageism is alive and well for both older and younger employees.

- Falling victim to previous employer bias. That is, believing that a job candidate who worked for a competitor or in a similar job in another company can and will fulfill the job responsibilities in your company. The same is true for people having a similar experience as the interviewer (e.g., veteran, losing home in wildfire).

- Not candid about or misrepresenting the company's culture. It's why candidates and employees leave without saying "good-bye!"

- Not taking the time to build trust during the interview and selection process, and not following-through on promises made. Remember, job candidates can become future customers or vendors, or may be in a position to award contracts ... or not, based on their experiences during this selection process!

- Use of nonqualified assessments during the preemployment process. These will result in misfits in the job. Remember, anything used during "preemployment" is considered part of the "preemployment process" and is subject to legal ramifications (e.g., violation of employment practices, charges of discrimination).

- Ignoring questions or skipping around in a structured interview format, making it difficult to compare candidates. You also lose a good defense for any internal company or outside employment challenges.

- Believe anyone's job performance issue can be "fixed" with coaching, training, and motivation. The problem is that someone who is a poor fit for the job will not work that hard, and neither will you!

- Failing to share the real expectations for the position to ensure the candidates are aware, able, and willing to do all that is required (e.g., travel; manage a dysfunctional team; flexible hours; meet quarterly metrics for projects or sales; work with remote teams in different time zones).

- Ask questions that cannot be asked legally. Example: "This job requires 25% travel – are you able to do that?" (good) versus "Will your kids be OK with you being gone?" (illegal)

Now that you've become aware, it's time to conduct effective interviews!

Notes ...

Notes ...

13

Conduct a Phone Screen Interview

A Phone Screen Interview is conducted for several reasons:

- To assess the quality of the applicant's phone or video skills.

- To ensure the person's interests, experience and skills meet the needs of the position.

- To provide a way to determine the level of salary and benefits required by the applicant. Note: If the applicant asks about salary range, keep it realistic. For example, if the company range is $5,000 to $8,000 per month, but the company only wants to pay $6,000, offer a salary range of $5,500 to $6,500. Remember everyone want the highest number.

- To save time and money. Allows you to filter out people who clearly do not meet the qualifications for the job, regardless of what is written on their resumes.

Review Prescreening Questions completed by candidate on your ATS. Also, review Core Value Assessment and Job Skills Test results if required at this point. (IF they are required and the applicant did not complete, do NOT proceed until they are finished. There is usually a reason despite the excuse they provide.) Check with assessment vendor as to when the assessment can be administered and results used.

A job candidate did not complete the core value assessment, citing she didn't have time during the application process. Tasha, the business owner, conducted her Phone Screen Interview anyway and loved the responses the candidate gave, but requested the candidate complete the core value assessment before she would proceed. The core value results (direct admission) indicated she'd taken $10,000 from her previous employer. If Tasha had followed her own system, she would not be in the difficult position of letting the person know she was no longer a viable candidate after expressing positive interest in her.

When you conduct the Phone Screen Interview:

- Get actual dates of hire (first and last days worked) for the listed employment history.

- Ask or verify the salary or wages s/he is seeking.

- Get the applicant's specific reason for leaving each prior position. Steer clear of delving into personal reasons for gaps in employment.

- When possible, ask the interview questions provided in the candidate's assessment report to clarify the person's fit with the job.

Why is this information important?

- When you get the specific employment dates, you will see how much work experience a person actually has.

- When you ask for the person's desired salary (or hourly wage), you can determine if it fits in your compensation guidelines.

- If the person is seeking a better job, different job responsibilities, or a better job title, you can discern if that is possible in your company. A job title can be misleading or too vague. Be crystal clear here about job specifics, then ask if s/he is still interested.

It is important to really listen to why a person left his/her previous employer(s).

I remember interviewing a woman for an operations manager position with a R&D company. She had the experience and credentials. However, she had worked for three other companies during a short period of time. There appeared to be a pattern. When I asked why she had left each one and really listened to the heart of the issue, I found a similar reason for all three times. She didn't like to be told what to do.

When I asked her if she had noticed a pattern as to why she left each job, she said, "No."

We reviewed the reasons she had given to me and the details of the position. I indicated that it would be no different with this company. She was very appreciative and responded that she didn't wish to continue making the same mistake! She told me that now she'd be looking at different options for future employment. Unfortunately, not everyone is so conscientious.

Be aware of how an applicant handles these questions. It is an indication of how s/he will handle concerns or mistakes in the future with your employees, clients, vendors, and community. After you've verified the employment dates, noted the person's desired salary or wages, and reason for leaving his/her employer(s), the next question to ask is: "Tell me about yourself and your professional background."

This is an important question since it:

- Provides the framework for the job candidate's interest in the position.

- Shows the amount of research they've conducted on the company.

- Reveals his/her level of preparation for the interview.

Ask the questions in a way that will ensure you get professional information, not personal information (e.g., number of kids, marital status). Personal information can now or later be construed as discriminatory. If the person does provide personal information, do not write it down. Remind the interviewee that you're interest is in his/her qualifications and work experience relative to the position being offered.

This is the opportunity to clarify the expectations and goals of the position. Companies today are seeking employees that can hit the floor running and are eager to learn.

Notes ...

14

Conduct a Face-to-Face Interview
Super sharpen your interview results

Conduct interviews with job candidates when all objective data has been obtained (e.g., assessments, skill testing, background checks, education verifications).

The goal is to select the three best qualified candidates who could be given a job offer.

Wise hiring managers have narrowed the hiring pool down to five or six top candidates. Interviewing more than this number indicates you've not done a good job with Phone Screen Questions or have not attracted enough qualified candidates that meet minimum requirements. If this has happened, go back and start over to see what was missed. Putting a band-aid on an issue will not provide the solution of hiring amazing employees.

Important! Before Moving Forward ...

Select three to five other people to conduct interviews with you as a group or individually.

It's critical everyone is on the same page by using the strategic selection system!

There are many examples of group interviews erupting into conflict due to self-interests (e.g., wanting a friend, woman, or person of color to be selected) or because of individual interviewers voicing complaints about the company or job. Be sure these issues are addressed privately and not aired during the interview.

The key person conducting the interviews and making the final decision should be the boss. Others are there to contribute their opinions and share any information not previously covered.

Very Important Note for Management and Executive Positions

Plan to have additional conversations with the top candidates to ensure they are the right leaders for your company. While many job candidates at this level are well-versed in what to say, their true personality, industry and company perspectives, and ability to work with and through others usually shows up in these conversations. So create additional interview questions but keep the initial questions the same for each candidate. Don't be afraid to learn more about why s/he wants to work for your company and with you. Use Drill Down Method. What value can s/he bring to your employees and customers?

Ready? It's Time to Conduct a Full Interview!

Open the Interview:

- Build rapport. While it's important to help the person feel comfortable, s/he is there for an interview. Set the applicant at ease with coffee or water. The purpose is to have him/her be less guarded with answers.

- Set the agenda/timetable. Be sure this is communicated to the applicant prior to the actual interview so s/he is prepared to complete the entire process you have designed for the meeting. (Remember, it's the company's responsibility to inform the applicant of the amount of time required for the interview.)

The Body of the Interview:

- Prior to the interview, review the candidate's information already obtained. Plan to clarify any discrepancies to ensure you have the correct information. This is a critical part of the process and establishes the quality of the interview results and future relationship with the job candidate.

- Review the answers to the Phone Screen Questions, even if you personally conducted it.

Now you have the facts in hand and it can be a very telling part of the interview.

- How does the interviewee handle your questions?

- If s/he is trying to hide something, it will usually come out during this process.

- If s/he has changed her or his mind about how to answer a question, you will gain some insight as to how s/he may handle on-the-job situations when a mistake has been made or a lie discovered.

- Be prepared to really listen to the answers. Don't be afraid to repeat your question or the candidate's answer to clarify the facts. Remember, you're asking relevant questions that can reveal if the person:

  - Can do the job?
  - Will do the job?
  - Can do the job successfully here?

- Ask job relevant questions contained in the structured interview format. Focus on whether the person can and will perform the specific tasks of the job. What previous results were achieved? Challenges resolved? Mistakes handled? Since a majority of applicants stretch the truth in their resumes, this is your opportunity to clarify.

- Do NOT ask about the latest book read or the last movie s/he saw. They are not job relevant—unless, of course, you are hiring for a school, book publisher, or movie producer!

- At the end of the interview, it's critical that you are clear about the quality of the person's skills and the areas needing further development. That's the purpose of a good interview.

- Listen and take appropriate notes. Write down only the facts. Don't cover up what you're writing down or write while the applicant is talking. Simply wait until s/he has completed her or his comments and then write down a couple of words to remind you of the answers.

- Don't forget to ask the interview questions contained in the core value assessment and job fit assessment to uncover additional information and insights. Whenever possible, review these questions during the Phone Screen Interview.

The Close of the Interview:

Ask the candidate if s/he has any questions.

- Be wary of the person with no questions! This reveals a lack of preparation and/or a belief s/he understands the job. That's usually not the case!

- Clarify job expectations upfront (e.g., work days and hours, travel, remote work availability).

- Describe the position. Note that this should be done *after* you've asked the interview questions. If you describe the position sooner, the candidate will only tell you what you wish to hear. At the beginning of the interview, you can include a general, one-line statement about the position to ensure that you and the candidate are discussing the same job.

- If the candidate appears to be a better fit for a different job, ask if s/he would be interested in it. Take responsibility to ensure the information is forwarded to that hiring manager. Follow through!

- Let the candidate know what's next. Ask for any additional information you may need. Tell the candidate when you expect to receive this information and when s/he can expect your decision.

- Follow through! (I cannot stress this enough.)

A True Story about why many companies hurt their reputations by lack of follow through as promised.

A woman interviewed for a Director of Quality Assurance position with a fast-growing Tier-Three automotive supplier. She fit the job requirements well. The interviewer was interested and promised a job offer in two weeks. The two weeks came and went without any word from the interviewer, and he did not return her calls.

In the meantime, the woman was offered a job with a Tier-One automotive company as a Purchasing Manager. She accepted.

In her new role, she was responsible for vetting potential suppliers to determine if their proposed RFQ (Request for Quote) met their quality standards. When it came time to determine the Tier-Three automotive supplier's status, she said "No." She informed them that, "If you're unable to keep your word with job applicants, how can we rely on you to keep your word with us?" The company did not get the contract!

Remember, job candidates are future customers and vendors. They do influence friends, families, and business associates about your company and have long memories! Leave them with a favorable impression of your company, even if the answer is "no." (Yes! I've mentioned this often throughout this book because we forget or overlook the impact we have on our businesses when interviewing job candidates!)

The interview is one of your opportunities to WOW! them, even though you may not be able to hire them. If you treat your prospective and current employees being considered for new job opportunities well, they will be your best advocates for your company. If you don't, they will tell many more people about their bad experiences!

Remember, the interviews are one-third of the selection decision!

Notes ...

Notes ...

15

Using Qualified Assessments and Skill Testing

Suggestions to save time . . .

- Have the core value assessment and skill testing completed prior to the Phone Screen Interview.

- Have the job fit assessment completed prior to the full interview.

When possible, having assessments and skill testing completed prior to the interview reduces interviewer bias because you've collected and reviewed objective and reliable data.

Check with the vendor and review the technical manual for how and when these can be used.

Example, some honesty/integrity assessments cannot be used on current employees. But these assessments are important for preemployment purposes since they provide direct-admissions information not found in public records. (See Chapter 9: Use the Right Assessments and Skill Tests.)

Check with the third-party vendor and the technical manual about the best method to use with these all-important tools. Remember, assessments are one-third of the selection decision and interviews are one-third of the selection decision! Now, it's time for the last one-third of the selection decision ... due diligence.

Notes ...

Notes ...

Part 3

Third Side of Selection Triad: Due Diligence

Due diligence is one-third of the selection decision.

- Chapter 16: Purpose of Completing a Full Due Diligence

- Chapter 17: Types of Checks, Records Used, and the Purpose of Being Thorough
  - Employment, Education, and Professional License Verifications
  - Conduct Professional Reference Checks

16

Purpose of Completing a Full Due Diligence

Many interviewers falsely believe they only have to look into the whites of someone's eyes to know whether or not that person is telling the truth. The reality? Interviewers have a very small chance of differentiating lies from facts during an interview for a variety of reasons (e.g., failing to use Drill Down Method (page 122), distractions).

It is important because it's pay now or pay later! You're giving them the keys and knowledge about your business, customers, and products/services. So, it's crucial that you've completed a full due diligence.

Remember, a well-designed due diligence process provides protection for current employees, clients, and the company. I recommend using a third-party vendor to ensure it's handled consistently each time and that legal statutes are followed.

Reminder: There have been several warnings to have three top candidates! Many times, the #1 candidate has an issue during this part of the Selection Triad or declines the job offer! If you have three top candidates, you can readily move on to the second or third candidate without needing to start over.

If you haven't done so already, now's the time to conduct a thorough due diligence.

Because of the interviews and review of assessments and testing (qualified job fit, skills, and/or core value assessments), you believe you have a good picture of who this person is. But be wary! *The person may be a sheep in wolf's clothing! Or, keeping with the car analogy, it may be a lemon ... looks great on the outside and is priced at the level you want to pay, but it has too many mechanical issues.*

Remember, the goal is to collect enough of the right (consistent, objective, reliable, and valid) information to make good selection decisions.

To prevent surprises or lawsuits later:

- Obtain background check, credit records, and other job-relevant records (e.g., driving, social security).

- Verify employment, education, and professional licensing information.

- Talk with professional references.

Be sure the information requested is job-related and the request for that data includes all appropriate candidates at the same time during the selection process (e.g., candidates being given face-to-face interviews).

Remember, it's pay now or pay later ... white collar crime is on the rise! So, it's prudent to include everyone, regardless of his/her level in a company!

There are many executives that will not talk with job candidates without the data already being compiled before their interview!

Still not convinced?

A bad hire can negatively impact your bottom line ranging from one to five times the salary of the employee and that figure may not reflect the intangible costs of litigation or loss of valuable clients and other employees. (You may need to update your hiring calculator!)

Conduct an online search for "negligent hiring cases." It will awaken you to the fact that it can cost employers millions of dollars, customers, and the safety and well-being of company employees.

Here are the most common "lies" and how to verify them:

- List degrees or credentials that they have not earned. *Conduct education verifications.*

- Job titles and job responsibilities are inflated. *When conducting employment verifications, ask about title and job responsibilities.* Some will invent employers, and many will alter reasons for leaving. Contact all previous employers listed! If someone does not return your call, there may be a good reason.

- Criminal records camouflaged. They may slightly alter the spelling of their name or date of birth. Some will simply extend the dates of employment with the employer prior to incarceration. *Get a copy of the person's driver's license to ensure spelling and date of birth. Verify actual dates of employment with each previous employer.*

- Dates of employment are often misleading. Many applicants will use years, not actual dates, on resumes. Again, a fully completed application form will help. *Require all dates be completed. Do NOT allow the applicant to use "See Resume."*

Notes ...

Notes ...

17

Types of Checks, Records Used, and the Purpose of Being Thorough

- **Background checks.** Companies are liable for any harm due to an employee's negligent acts.

- **Credit checks.** If the job candidate will have access to confidential financial details, cash, or assets, it is important to know about his/her financial background.

- **Driving records.** Companies are held liable for employees when they drive for business purposes.

- **Drug testing and medical.** These routine procedures ensure a safe workplace and provide baseline data in the event of alleged workplace accidents.

- **Social Security traces.** Provide names (including AKAs or aliases) and addresses associated with the social security number that can be broadened to check on criminal history.

Unfortunately, many hiring managers, in their rush to get the person hired, overlook this crucial part of the due diligence process or do an incomplete job of it, opening the door for serious legal problems!

Again, having a third-party vendor conduct these checks for each and every job candidate, regardless of level within the company, ensures objectivity and a faster turnaround time since they do this work often.

Employment, Education, and Professional License Verifications

Most companies falsely believe they conduct reference checks, when, in fact, it's only an employment verification. It's vital to understand the difference.

All parts of each candidate's background are important to verify. They ensure the applicant has the qualifications, education, and experience required for the position.

- **Employment:** Call the applicant's former employers and verify actual dates of employment, title of his/her position, and title of position of his/her immediate supervisor. The employer(s) probably will not verify much else!

- **Education:** Confirm the education, degree, training, or certification claims by contacting the issuing institution or company.

- **Professional License:** Same as Education.

- **Reference Checks:** Contact professional references and use the suggested Reference Check Questions provided in Chapter 10.

Be sure to have the applicant sign release documentation to ensure privacy and reduce liability issues.

Conduct Professional Reference Checks

Conducting reference checks is one of your final chances to discover anything you want to know before selecting a person for the job. This includes talking with coworkers, vendors, and others when wanting to do a job transfer or promote a person, or when hiring a contractor or consultant as an employee!

The key is to ask for a list of five professional references. Have the job candidate contact them to let them know you or a company representative will contact them. A side benefit in requesting that the applicant reach out to their references is how well the applicant follows directions! (If the person is surprised by your call, the applicant probably didn't follow through!)

Reference checks are an excellent way of ascertaining who this person is from another professional person's perspective. Most people are forthcoming in their responses since they have been asked to participate by the former employee. The typical call can take five to ten minutes and save you countless hours. It's best to have a third-party conduct these inquiries since they will be more objective and provide you with the facts.

Reminder: You want the applicant to provide managers or professional-level coworkers as references. Make sure you specifically ask for them.

Exercise caution with reference letters. You don't know their true origin or the real reason why they were written. Forgeries do occur. A common concern is if they were written as an agreement so the person wouldn't sue them. Ninety-nine percent of reference letters only speak well of the person and it's impossible to read between the lines. If you accept these letters, contact the signer and conduct the same formal reference check as you would for other candidates.

Wise advice: Conduct internal reference checks!
I remember being told a story about a "well-liked" guy being given a promotion. The problem? He was only "well-liked" by his boss! Normally, he was very rude and condescending to his coworkers and vendors.
If the company had done an "internal reference check" of its employee, the company would not have promoted him. Instead, the company could have offered him leadership development training and an executive coach. As a result, the company lost top talent, several customers, and eventually had to fire him.

For a new hire, rehire, or consultant/contractor/ temp, talk with the people the person works with currently, and also previous bosses and coworkers, clients, vendors, suppliers, and community leaders who have directly worked with the person during the past five to ten years. Stay away from his/her family, friends, or neighbors who will tell you what you want to hear or how green or brown the person's lawn is!

If you've followed the selection process as outlined in *Hire Amazing Employees, Revised Edition*, **it is unlikely that you will find out anything that will prevent you from hiring this person at this point.** However, there are many companies that have overlooked this part of due diligence and have had to pay the price through termination, lawsuits or discrimination claims, and loss of top talent and customers.

Notes ...

Part 4

The Job Offer and Employee Onboarding, The Basics

18

Additional Considerations to Address before Selecting the Top Three Candidates

Job Transferring or Promoting Internal Job Candidates

When you give a current employee a job transfer or job promotion without following a strategic selection system, it can result in the biggest unrecognized expense for most employers. The reason? If the person fails, s/he will not only take other top talent with him/her, but also some of your great customers may leave too!

All bosses want to keep top talent. But what happens when the person is not ready for greater responsibility, but threatens to leave without the job transfer or promotion? It may be in the company's best interest to let the person go. OR, have the employee complete a job fit assessment to determine his/her job fit for the new position or other positions in your company. If it looks good, then offer the employee the training and development required to be a top contender for the next job opening.

Addressing an Employee's Need for New Responsibilities

When bosses want to keep an employee who has asked for more responsibility, it's not a good idea to just give the person additional work on top of his/her current job responsibilities. Instead, review the work that needs to be done. Restructure the job based on his/her job fit assessment. There may be job duties that would be job enhancement opportunities for coworkers. Remember, it's not about giving the employee more work when s/he is already feeling overworked. It's about restructuring the department to focus and develop on each team member's strengths.

Job Transferring or Promoting Your Best Person

Your best person may not be the best manager or executive.

Example: The best sales person will most likely not be a strong support manager, administrator, or visionary CEO. What the person is good at is selling. Support, encourage, and pay the employee well to keep him/her in the role s/he excels. Don't give your employee the keys to a different desk.

A woman was a top salesperson within her organization. The company decided to make her a manager in charge of the administrative sales group to help improve the interactions between customer service

and the sales group. She failed miserably. Instead of
offering her the original job back, they fired her!
The company lost several key customers too!

This scenario happens all too often in our zest to save money or promote someone! It is understandable to want to keep someone who wants to be promoted, but they may not be ready for that level of responsibility or have a clear idea of what the new job demands. Take time to use the information in *Hire Amazing Employees, Revised Edition* to help you determine the true potential success of a person. Otherwise, it will become a costly loss of the employee, clients, and other top performers.

Moving Consultant or Contractor to Full- or Part-Time Employment

When you hire a contractor or consultant as a full- or part-time employee, there can be a subtle change in the relationship. As the boss, be mindful of how you listen to the person who is now an employee. There are times bosses are not as respectful to employees and their ideas as they are to consultants.

Have this conversation upfront. It's better to keep the person in a 1099 role instead of hiring him/her and creating issues. If the reason the person wants to become an employee is to access company benefits or other perks or bonuses, provide the funds for the person to purchase these on his/her own or update the person's contract to include perks and/or bonuses.

Amanda, a finance consultant, wanted to become a full-time employee. She was recommended by the company's business consultant, Joe, to help the company clean up some accounting issues. But Amanda wanted a job full-time and told the president of the company she could save the company a lot of money by getting rid of Joe. The problem was that Amanda did not have the experience or insight to resolve the internal people challenges. She created a lot of brouhaha and was put on a performance improvement plan. She was let go three months later!

Alternative to Full-Time Employment

(e.g., part-time, temporary, or contract position; and on-site, remote, or hybrid)

Some job applicants no longer need to work full-time, but are reluctant to retire or have become more selective in the types of work they will do and the types of bosses they will work for. Set aside any biases (e.g., ageism) and interview the person just like you would anyone else. You'll be surprised by his/her abilities and willingness to get the job done.

Experienced employees can make good coaches and trainers to help other people develop necessary skills. Again, use your strategic selection system to ensure job fit.

A retired not-for-profit president still wanted to work. A wise CEO from another not-for-profit hired her. The CEO explained to the newly hired director, "I want you to coach and develop my current team. They have a lot of skills and need someone to mentor them to excel." It was a win-win-win for everyone.

If the person wants to transition to onsite or remote work (or a hybrid), be sure s/he understands what is involved. Not everyone can work remotely or be comfortable working onsite after working virtually. Be clear about expectations and use your strategic selection system and job fit assessment. If everything is looking good, offer a three-month trial to ensure it'll work out. You don't want to lose a good employee.

George was a current employee who wanted to live in New York state. He offered his boss the chance to open up new sales opportunities in the New York market as an outside sales rep. As an inside sales rep, his numbers were good. But before his boss agreed to the plan, the company used its strategic selection system and job fit assessment, which showed that George would not fit the job responsibilities required to open up a new sales market. So, the company created a new pathway for George to still be able to move and work as an off-site inside sales rep while living in New York state.

Notes ...

Notes ...

19

The Job Offer

Many qualified job candidates have a "must-have list" to be fulfilled before they agree to work for you and accept your job offer. Be willing to negotiate within reason. Put any agreements into writing and include them in the job offer letter for the job candidate to sign.

A red flag that often gets in the way and causes lawsuits later is when promises are made, but not kept, and not included in the job offer letter.

The moment you've been working to achieve!

You've done the work! Found three top contenders! Now, it's time to make the job offer. I would recommend making it via a phone call first. If the candidate accepts the job offer, or expresses an interest in doing so, follow up with a job offer letter that needs to be signed and returned within three to five days.

The purpose of a job offer letter is to ensure there are no surprises later based upon promises made during the interviews or during job offer negotiations. *For example, if you promised to pay relocation expenses, the specifics need to be outlined in the job offer letter.*

The reason for the three to five days is to limit the candidate from using your job offer to negotiate a better job offer with a different company or his/her current employer.

Here are some pointers:

- Have your attorney, business manager, and/or human resource professional draft the letter to ensure consistency. Top performers want to work with companies who are in compliance.

- Follow legal employment guidelines to determine when you can provide the job offer letter to your top candidate (e.g., before or after medical review and/or drug testing).

- Outline benefits, special agreements, and/or promises to prevent misunderstandings and litigation later (e.g., work requirements, work hours, relocation, special equipment, additional time-off, health care, pay increase in three months).

- Be sure to include in your job offer letter an overview of the benefits package and when each benefit is effective. These benefits can make up an additional 20-35% or more of a full compensation package. It's one of the top reasons job candidates will choose to work for you over a different job offer, especially if your company has a reputation of not slashing benefits when the economy shifts.

- A well-written job offer letter can provide documentation in the event of any dispute.

- While there are websites offering job offer letters or employment agreement "forms," work with an attorney to write your own. Form letters often have provisions that are not relevant for your company and are difficult for anyone reading them to understand. These form letters often hurt your company's reputation.

- If job candidate uses your job offer to negotiate better pay or promotion with his/her current employer, do not negotiate. Move on to the next candidate(s). Note: Studies have shown these employees rarely stay with their current employer for more than six months. Why? Money and other perks are not the real cause of their job dissatisfaction.

- If the letter has been signed, but the job candidate changes his/her mind, let the person go. Do not negotiate. Encourage the person to do what is best for him/her.

- If the candidate chooses not to accept the job offer, keep the door and the lines of communication open for when you have future openings!

- How you handle this final leg of the Selection Triad can impress a candidate who is more likely to think favorably of your company even if they decide to decline your job offer. And yes, this happens more often than you think!

- If you need to rescind a job offer after it's been accepted, consider seeking other opportunities for the displaced person, especially if the newly hired person has been relocated or recruited from a previous job. Review the workload, client demands, and upcoming employee changes (medical leaves). What other work can the person do while s/he seeks other employment? Contractual or short-term? Positive employee relations go a long way!

Notes ...

Notes ...

20

The Success of a New Hire Is Up to You!

The success of a new hire relies largely on the boss! That's you! If you've done a good job following your well-designed strategic selection system as outlined in *Hire Amazing Employees, Revised Edition,* you should feel comfortable and confident that you've hired the right person for the right job.

But ... if along the way, you've made an error, don't compound it by thinking you can train, coach, or motivate the person to be someone different. Simply follow your company's system for exiting the person.

You've made the job offer and it has been accepted. It's time to ensure the person is welcomed, has all s/he needs to succeed, and that both of you are on the same page! The job candidate (and you) will forget much that was said during a selection interview. So, even if you fear sounding like a parrot, it's important to review your expectations.

Create an employee onboarding program and fine-tune it to ensure your new hire is successful. Check with the Society for Human Resource Management (SHRM) and Association for Talent Development (ATD) for best practices.

Consider the following information to get started.

The job offer letter has been signed. Here's what needs to happen next:

- Have all benefits, payroll, and other documents signed (these can be done online with a designated person available to review the material and answer any questions). Plan to have this completed before the new hire's first day on the job.

- Several days ahead of time, provide information about parking, entrance to the building, dress, and the person that will greet him/her. Or, if remote, have a person or team ready to greet the new hire online, and ensure that all materials, along with user name(s) and passwords(s), are readily available. Also, ensure any physical items that were express shipped have arrived and are set up properly.

- Assign different team members to take the new hire to lunch and join the new employee for breaks.

- For on-site hires: show them the location of the restrooms, coffee and snacks, and desk or work station. Have desk, computer, login information, and other equipment already available.

- Walk the new hire to the training room for employee orientation and onboarding.

- Have a meeting with the boss scheduled to review 180-Day Success Plan and expectations and to answer any questions on day one. This sets a positive tone!

- If there will be a mentor and/or coach, schedule 1:1 time accordingly and make that part of the 180-Day Success Plan.

Employee Onboarding Overview

A well-designed onboarding program can leave a new employee feeling engaged, confident, and happy to be an employee of your company.

As the boss, arrange your schedule either in person 1:1 or use a video conferencing platform to welcome the person. Use a multidepartment onboarding team and track his/her progress.

The success of a new employee is largely determined by how well s/he adjusts to the company and coworkers, and how well the organization's ethics, vision, mission and practices have been communicated. Remember, many times your perception of what you (and others) said during the interview process may not be what was heard or remembered!

In a study conducted by Corporate Executive Board, 50-70% of executives are failing within 18 months of taking on a role, regardless of whether they were an external hire or promoted from within. So it is critical that you provide all the needed support for the person to succeed.[10]

As the boss, you have the responsibility to acclimate your new hires, job transfers, and job promotions to ensure their and your success.

- Provide them appropriate resources.

- After learning how the company operates (especially employees being transferred or promoted), encourage them to take initiative within company guidelines.

- Remind them it is their responsibility to ask for clarification and help.

Doing a great job of interviewing will not ensure the new employee's success unless you provide a well-designed onboarding program.

Take time, starting with the first hour of his/her employment, to review everything! But don't do it all at once.

Spread it out over the course of one to two weeks, depending on the position. Your current customers, vendors, and employees' families benefit from your efforts to ensure the new hire fully understands the current company and its culture, especially if any future company, employee, customer, product, or service changes are planned.

First, review the 180-Day Success Plan. Remember, this was designed as a game plan for the person's success. Set clear goals and metrics. Require the new hire to provide you with a focused action plan for your review. It's an excellent opportunity to share and reinforce company information, client needs, and company policies. Although you may be clear as to your expectations, s/he may not be clear about the steps to be taken to achieve those goals. Be sure to discuss the pros and cons of any differing points-of-view and get on the same page.

Second, discuss the "Honeymoon Period." This period can last a couple of hours, days, weeks, or months. It normally ends when an issue occurs that was unexpected and creates an "elephant" if not addressed immediately. While the employee may wish to have the "honeymoon period" last, it limits the person from fully doing his or her job. Remember, most new hires are too careful when talking with clients, take longer than necessary to make decisions, fear being fired, and/or seek consensus before handling emergencies. These are examples of behaviors that can limit someone's success as a new person in the job.

Third, remind the new hire to learn how your company conducts business before making any changes. It requires about thirty days to learn the company's culture and systems or to learn his/her new job and expectations if it is a job transfer or promotion. For the next sixty to ninety days, any recommendations should be reviewed by you prior to implementation to ensure the design and execution fit within the company's standards.

This is especially true for executives. Too many times, they want to bring in their own people or implement their own way of doing things right away. This is very disruptive since no two companies operate exactly the same way!

Also, if you want someone to be fired, do it before the new leader starts. Otherwise, give the new leader an opportunity to get to know the current staff and their work abilities before s/he recommends any job changes, or the hiring or exiting of people. Then, follow the strategic selection system for any and all hires and job transfers!

Sally started her new job on a Monday, excited to be working for a company that had a great selection process. But she learned an hour after arriving that her boss was too busy to talk with her until later in the week.

Todd was assigned to get her started and to show her where everything was located (e.g., office, laptop, passwords, rest rooms, lunch room). But he didn't know much about her job duties. He could only help get the items she needed for her desk.

The previous person in her position had left the company. She learned he'd been fired, even though her new boss had said he'd left to pursue other interests during the interview.

So, Sally started talking with her new team and coworkers in different departments. Everyone had a different point-of-view as to what her priorities should be. Then, her vice president and his boss (the CEO) each had conversations with her, but offered different opinions about where her focus should be.

On Friday afternoon she resigned, clearly frustrated by the lack of a cohesive onboarding process.

The Basics

Checklist Ideas for Professional and Management Hires:

- Have an onboarding program that begins on the person's first day and lasts over the first six months (180 days), with weekly reviews, and special attention to activities and accomplishments during the first 10 days on the job.

- Be sure all paperwork is completed before the new hire's first day.

- Have someone be responsible for introductions to key people, coworkers, and all people on the person's team.

- Encourage the new employee to schedule time with key people and coworkers in different departments to learn more about the company and its customers, internally and externally.

- Set up lunches and/or meetings with key people, coworkers, and team members during the first couple of weeks.

- Ensure there is time during the first week to spend 1:1 with each team member.

- Set up client and company location visits.

- **Remind the new employee to listen more than talk.** Note: This is where many employees in new positions get in trouble. They attend these meetings not to listen and learn, but to state what they will be doing and changes they will be making in the future. Coach the person to only ask questions at this point. Let him/her know it may be too soon for sharing.

- Identify a mentor that the new person can ask company and industry questions and discuss problems encountered.

- If the person will have a coach, make sure the introduction is made and expectations for coaching are outlined before the new employee is hired. Not everyone sees the value of having a coach or is coachable.

- Have video and written materials ready so the new hire can dive deeper into the company's products and/or services.

- Review company etiquette, history, mission, values, and communications.

- Review other departments and the company's other locations' organization chart(s), purpose(s) and goal(s).

- Review the company's policies and procedures and employee handbook topic by topic. Don't rely on the employee to read something new and easily understand how it works within your company. Do this over the course of days or weeks.

- Modify the above for job transfers and job promotions. Rehires should be treated as new hires.

- Create a separate training program for hourly and administrative people to learn more about the company and its products and services and to meet other team members. Also, provide them criteria for career advancement opportunities.

During and after 180 days for Professional and Management Hires

- Follow up weekly on the 180-Day Success Plan. What's working and what's not working? Don't overlook issues since these can grow from molehills into mountains when someone is off track.

- Use a qualified 360-degree feedback assessment to get structured insights from coworkers, boss(es), and employees. Remember to keep respondents' names confidential. This is used to gauge the new person's effectiveness and then provide laserlike coaching. Repeat after 60 days.

- Provide written feedback on performance, including areas that are working well and areas for improvement. Be sure this is an interactive process that meets the company's needs and the employee's professional development goals. *There should never be surprises or old issues brought up during annual or semi-annual performance reviews!*

- The new hire cannot succeed as a "lone ranger" and must be able to work with and through his/her team(s) to achieve intended results. If the person has a coach, ensure specific issues are being addressed by asking the person, "What did your coach say?"

- Set up new goals, and refine existing ones based on the person's career path, leadership development needs, and/or managing people/ project management challenges. Don't forget to include feedback from 360-degree assessment and other feedback when designing future training and development needs.

  - **Career Opportunities for Advancement.** Share with each employee and design, along with the employee, individual career opportunities. Do NOT make assumptions as to the best career path for a person without asking and listening to their desires and goals first.

  - **Leadership Development** is important for everyone, whether or not s/he will become a boss or project manager (e.g., financial analysis, critical thinking, emotional intelligence, diversity, resolving conflict).

  - **Managing People and Project Management Development.** Provide now, before the person is promoted or given new opportunities. S/he won't have the energy, band-width, or ability to absorb the "fire hose" approach after being given the position!

- Create a separate career advancement plan for hourly and administrative employees that meets their needs. They are just as important!

Remember, your ability to provide the training and development your employees need will determine your own options for career advancement! Make your employees and their skill development your #1 priority!

Notes ...

Notes ...

End Notes

[1] "Selecting Selection Tools – a Map Through the Maze," John W. Howard, PhD, CEO & Founder of Performance Resources, Inc.

[2] "85 Percent of Job Applicants Lie on Resumes. Here's How to Spot a Dishonest Candidate," INC.

[3] "Should You Trust Your Gut in Hiring Decisions?" Society of Human Resource Management.

[4] "Delivering through Diversity," McKinsey & Company.

[5] *Harvard Business Review* study where they followed 360,000 people through their careers during a period of 20 years and found that a key ingredient in retaining people is ensuring that they are matched to their jobs in terms of their abilities, interests, and personalities.

[6] "How to Develop a Job Description," Society of Human Resource Management.

[7] "85 Percent of Job Applicants Lie on Resumes. Here's How to Spot a Dishonest Candidate," INC.

[8] "Testing and Assessment: An Employee's Guide to Good Practices," US Department of Labor, Employment and Training Administration.

[9] *Harvard Business Review* study where they followed 360,000 people through their careers during a period of 20 years and found that a key ingredient in retaining people is ensuring that they are matched to their jobs in terms of their abilities, interests, and personalities.

[10] "Why Most New Executives Fail – And Four Things Companies Can Do About It," *Forbes.*

About the Author
and How to Work with the Jeannette

Straight talk with immediate results.

Jeannette Seibly has been hiring and firing for companies for more than forty years. The first fourteen years, she worked in corporate America for small and large corporations in human resources. During the past thirty years, Jeannette has worked as a business advisor and executive consultant, speaker, and author in North America and internationally, especially with small and family-owned businesses.

Hire Amazing Employees, Revised Edition was written as a guide for executives, business owners, entrepreneurs, family business leaders, and hiring managers in small companies ($1M to $30M) to get back to basics. A well-designed strategic selection system will improve retention, revenues, and results when followed and when the onboarding and company practices and policies have been updated too.

Small businesses, from a variety of industries, have used this information to reduce the number of hiring mistakes most businesses make—and many of their competitors continue to make. *Hire Amazing Employees, Revised Edition* provides additional value-added practices to include in every strategic selection system.

To learn more about Jeannette Seibly and her other products and services, visit her website at *SeibCo.com.*

Have questions? Let's Chat!

Contact Jeannette for a complimentary discussion.

- Management Consultant and Assessment Provider—Manage people for results, design strategic selection systems, and use qualified assessments for job fit.

- Facilitator—Transform outcomes with management teams, partnerships, and boards.

- Keynote Speaker—Award winning. Contact her for virtual or onsite customized presentations or workshops.

Additional Notes ...

Additional Notes ...

www.ingramcontent.com/pod-product-compliance
Lightning Source LLC
Chambersburg PA
CBHW060318030426
42336CB00011B/1110